Business Guide to Japan

Opening Doors . . . and Closing Deals!

Boye De Mente is an acknowledged authority on the Orient and the author of more than 30 books, including the first books ever on the Japanese way of doing business— *Japanese Etiquette & Ethics in Business* (1960) and *How to Do Business with the Japanese* (1962). He first came to Japan in 1949 with the U.S. Army Security Agency and has been involved with Japan as a journalist, editor, lecturer, and writer ever since.

Other Books by Boye De Mente

Business Guide to Japan

Opening Doors . . . and Closing Deals!

by

Boye Lafayette De Mente

YENBOOKS are published and distributed
by the Charles E. Tuttle Company, Inc.
of Rutland, Vermont & Tokyo, Japan
with editorial offices at
2-6 Suido 1-chome, Bunkyo-ku, Tokyo 112

LCC Card No. 89-50662
ISBN 0-8048-1613-1

First edition, 1989
Third printing, 1991

Printed in Japan

Contents

Contents

Contents

Contents

Contents

Preface

Getting into the Game

One of the ways Japanese often use to measure foreign understanding of, appreciation for, and commitment to Japan is by whether or not the individuals concerned can eat *natto* (not-toe). The question is not if they *like* it but whether they are able to eat it (without getting sick).

Natto is a Japanese food made from fermented soybeans that looks terrible, smells awful and—to the unconditioned foreign palate—tastes like a batch of glue gone bad.

Japan's always outspoken critic-at-large Michihiro Matsumoto says that the best way to understand how Japan's business world works is to look at each company organization as a glob of *natto*. In fact, he describes *all* Japanese organizations, political, professional, and social as well as economic, as *natto* organisms.

Matsumoto makes several points with his pungent analogy:

1) Japanese companies are quintessentially *Japanese* and are therefore unlike companies in any other country.

11

2) Japanese companies have a distinctive character and flavor that only a *Japanese* can fully understand and accept.

3) And, foreigners who have not acquired a "taste" and appreciation for Japanese companies over a long period of time will inevitably find it difficult to deal with them.

One of the unique characteristics of Japan's *natto* companies is that they do not have permanently established, well-defined "doors" for dealing with outsiders, whether businessmen or the public at large. Each organization is more or less a gluey monolith that is difficult or impossible to penetrate using the typical, straightforward Western approach.

In Matsumoto's metaphorical company, when an outsider who has no inside connections tries to establish a relationship with the company—in the hope of doing business—he almost never penetrates the inner wall of the ball. When the outsider approaches the company it may "give" a little at the point of pressure, like a mushy balloon, and may bulge out somewhere else, but no permanent break is made in the company skin.

The only way a businessman, foreign *or* Japanese, can actually get through the company shell is for *someone on the inside to pull him in!*

As strained as this analogy might appear, it nevertheless offers valuable insights into the anatomy and character of the typical Japanese company. Unlike most Western companies with their revolving doors and welcome mats, the Japanese company tends to be a closed system that very carefully screens any "foreign body" that seeks entry, and then, if the alien body is not rejected by the system, it proceeds to "digest" it to make it compatible with the whole organ.

This homogenizing process is not something that can be done quickly. In fact, it is often the straw that defeats the impatient time-and-money-conscious foreign suitor.

While the Western company is generally open to approaches on many levels and is capable of many different kinds and levels of reactions, the typical Japanese company is usually not capable of flexibility, quick reactions, or any kind of spontaneity.

There is a specific, culturally sanctioned protocol for approaching and dealing with Japanese companies that is as structured as a mathematical equation. Generally, one cannot successfully establish contact and develop a business relationship with a Japanese company without following this protocol in the right order and in the right way.

This Quick-Guide to doing business with Japanese companies pinpoints the key steps in this protocol, and provides insights and guidelines for following it successfully.

1

The Strange Bedfellows

The first key to understanding and dealing with Japanese businessmen is recognizing that there are two categories of culture—one that is visible and tangible, and one that is invisible and cannot be touched. It is the invisible culture of Japan that sets the Japanese apart from other people and makes their way of doing business different and often difficult for others to understand and follow.

Cultural differences that distinguish Japanese businessmen from American and European businessmen are basic and extend across the board, from their values and the nature of their human relationships to how they go about accomplishing things. While Japan's invisible culture has been considerably diluted since the end of World War II in 1945, and continues to evolve, it remains the primary force in the Japanese political and economic systems.

Japanese beliefs and behavior are bound up in a series of key words that express their philosophy, describe their mind-set, and prescribe their way of doing things. The bedrock word is *amae* (ah-my), which refers to the idealized relationship between people—

one of absolute trust and love in which no one takes undue advantage of the other and all are united in a spiritual bond that transcends the mundane and the mean.

The second most important word in the lexicon of the Japanese way is *wa* (wah), which means "peace and harmony," and which is both an outgrowth of *amae* and an essential ingredient for its existence and application. Of course, neither of these principles has ever worked perfectly, but they have been and still are the national "ethic" of the Japanese.

The whole fabric of Japanese culture that grew out of the philosophies of Shintoism, Buddhism, Confucianism, and Daoism was shaped and colored by the principles of *amae* and *wa*, in particular the etiquette and ethics of interpersonal relationships from the highest authority down to the lowest laborer. These relationships, and their psychological offspring, are what give the Japanese business system its form and much of its essence.

Other factors that have played primary roles in the molding of the Japanese character (and greatly influenced their attitude toward foreigners and the way they conduct business), are the small size of Japan, its relative isolation from the rest of the world, the racial homogeneity of the people, their belief in the superiority of their way of *wa*, and their view of the outside world as an enemy to be kept at bay.

With the forced opening of Japan to the West in the

1850s by the United States, the national character of the Japanese was made even more complicated by the rapid development of an inferiority complex brought on by their exposure to the wealth and power of Western countries transformed by the industrial revolution. This new complex, intermingled with the rest of their invisible cultural heritage, continues to affect all of their attitudes and behavior toward foreigners, particularly in their business relationships.

While there are a growing number of Japanese who can think like and behave like Westerners, they are still the exception, and when dealing with fellow Japanese they must conform to the all-encompassing "Japanese way"—or find themselves even more isolated and disadvantaged than Westerners.

Probably the second most important key in dealing effectively with the Japanese is an understanding of the emotional factor in their makeup.

2

The Emotional Factor in Business in Japan

Part of the old stereotype of the Japanese was that they were both inscrutable and unemotional. As it turns out, the Japanese are more knowable than most people because their mind-set is far more precisely structured and homogenized. And as for regarding the Japanese as unemotional, that mistake has been the downfall of many an insensitive foreigner, not to mention the cause of a lot of trouble on the international front.

In fact, the Japanese are far more emotional than Americans and most other Westerners, again for very solid historical reasons. Most Westerners are used to a degree of frankness, candid criticism, slights and outright insults, and have developed a thick skin to counter such behavior. Most Westerners are also practiced in giving as good as they receive. Not the Japanese. Their cultural conditioning has been to totally avoid such behavior and to keep such a tight reign on their emotions that others would not know what they were thinking or feeling, especially in formal and business situations.

At the same time, the extraordinarily refined etiquette system that the Japanese developed, especially in the use of the ''proper'' level of language, made them extremely sensitive to the most subtle slights or rude behavior. Their skin was so thin, and they were so sensitive, that a brief look of disapproval flickering across a person's face was enough to devastate them or earn their undying wrath.

Japanese skin is now much thicker than what it was as late as the 1960s but it is still gossamer thin when compared to the typical American or European. Their emotional antennae are up high and on twenty-four hours a day, especially in their dealings with foreigners. And the problem of their emotional sensitivity is compounded where foreigners are concerned because as much as they may try, most Japanese will readily admit that associating with foreigners automatically makes them uncomfortable. Franker businessmen often say outright that they do not like foreigners and would not do business with them if they had a choice.

This means that in order to deal effectively with Japanese, particularly those who have not been de-Japanized by long exposure to foreigners, it is very important to treat them with special decorum. The Japanese recognize that most foreigners do not know their etiquette, and generally speaking go to what for them are extreme lengths in tolerating Western behavior that they find unpleasant. (But they often then find that the negative effect of putting up with Western behavior is accumulative, and that some kind of purging mechanism is needed!)

Unlike other areas of business where it might be desirable and justifiable to insist that the Japanese change their ways and accept the foreign approach, one cannot assault their emotions without there being some kind of reaction. Learning how to stroke and not provoke a Japanese businessman is part of the process of doing business with them.

Obviously some of the more conspicuous and

damaging things to avoid are appearances of racial or cultural superiority, failure to pay proper respect to Japanese customs and beliefs, and failure to express appreciation or gratitude when it is due. As the Japanese become more self-confident—and arrogant—there will come a time when even derogatory remarks about eating raw fish or other traditional Japanese dishes will be regarded as highly insulting, and affect business relationships—and will be taboo if you want to do business with the Japanese.

3

Overcoming a Growing Resentment Factor

By 1988 there were strong signs that the top segment of Japan's business community, in particular the huge trading companies, construction-development firms, and securities companies, were beginning to feel beleaguered by the mass of foreign businessmen trying to sell them something or obtain financing for one kind of project or another. What had begun as a trickle in the 1960s had developed into a torrent by the late 1970s. Everybody from presidents and state governors down to shady hucksters was trying to sell the Japanese something.

Some of these visitors to Japan came in with a lot of

political clout, resulting in promises by the government that did not set well with the private business sector, exacerbating their feeling that the world was trying to take unfair advantage of Japan. Many Japanese were beginning to feel like the generous and sympathetic victim constantly besieged by beggars looking for a handout. Their "charity" was not being appreciated and they began to tighten the purse strings and resent the beggars.

It is important that foreign businessmen wanting to do business in Japan, or with Japanese companies outside of Japan, be aware of this factor and take steps to prevent it from becoming an overriding influence in their dealings with the Japanese. The key to this is to structure a deal that is obviously as beneficial to the Japanese side as it is to the foreign side, if not in a direct monetary sense, at least in a social, political and/or cultural sense.

Despite Japan's experience and success abroad, the future of the country hinges on the Japanese overcoming a serious information and cultural gap that exists between themselves and the rest of the world—an obstacle that they cannot overcome by themselves. Any foreign venture that will contribute to a reduction of this gap and help in the process of internationalizing Japan is more likely to be looked upon favorably by a Japanese company. This point should certainly be emphasized in any approach to Japanese firms or to any government agency.

4

The Role of Group-Think

George Orwell must have had some familiarity with Confucianism or Japanese culture when he wrote *1984*. One of the Japanese cultural factors that brings Orwell's book to mind (perhaps incorrectly) is called *shudan ishiki* (shuu-dahn ee-she-kee), an old term that means something like "group-think," which is a key point to be aware of in any dealings with Japan.

Shudan ishiki is an important ingredient in the Japanese way of managing, especially in larger companies. The concept of group-think incorporates not only the idea that everyone should think alike. It also includes the idea that in any enterprise, the individual comes first and takes precedence over professional training or skill—meaning that personnel can be (and often are!) transferred from one job to another irrespective of the job skills involved.

The thinking is that the whole company works as a group and that skilled individuals will carry those who are inexperienced so that the firm continues to move forward. In larger companies, where individuals are regularly switched among sections and departments,

22

this works, as long as a section of eight or more people never gets more than one or two inexperienced staff at a time.

Still, the foreign businessman dealing with a Japanese company should be cautious about getting stuck with a section member who is new in the group, is not totally familiar with its work, and who may have no clout at all.

In smaller companies, the custom of transferring personnel from one job to another without regard for the skills involved—and for putting the newest and greenest personnel out in front to handle walk-in visitors or callers—can cause substantially more trouble for the outsider.

This invariably adds to the amount of time, and sometimes the confusion, involved in contacting and dealing with small firms—and is another reason why it is important to have the name of a responsible person in the Japanese company you are calling or visiting. By immediately giving the name of the individual whom you want to contact, you can avoid getting caught up in the mushy outer wall of the Japanese company bureaucracy.

But the effects of group-think go well beyond regarding the company as a single organism made up of virtually identical parts that are interchangeable. It also is responsible for the way the Japanese structure themselves in groups and act together as teams—and even for the way they behave in social situations.

5

The Faction Factor

One aspect of the group-think syndrome that has a fundamental influence on business in Japan and impacts both indirectly and directly on foreign businessmen dealing with the Japanese are the *habatsu* (hah-bot-sue) or "factions" that Japanese naturally form when they come together. Given a vertically structured feudal society based on lifelong loyalty to individual leaders from the emperor and shogun on down to the local construction boss, every leader and his followers as well as every boss and his workers tended to become a faction or closely knit group that acted in unison to achieve goals as well as to defend itself against competitors or predators.

This situation prevailed for centuries, making it more or less second nature for Japanese who come together for any purpose to automatically form factions that quickly take on distinguishable characteristics and that must be dealt with in a specific way if anything is to be accomplished.

The difference between a Japanese "faction" and a foreign "team," company section, or department is not structural. It has to do with the relationships between the individual members, their attitudes toward the group, and how the group functions. And this, of course, involves a great many other cultural traits, from the strong sanctions to enforce harmony and the diffusement of personal responsibility, to decision by consensus.

Japanese factions vary in size and makeup from a section or a department in a company or government agency to affiliations of companies and politicians. The point I want to make here is that, with respect to company factions, outside businessmen must keep in mind that they are dealing with a closely knit group, not with just the leader or boss or any of the individual members. This means quick, individually made decisions will not be forthcoming; that all members of the group have the right to ask questions and express opinions, and that, in principle at least, everyone takes part in all final decisions.

The operation of a section (faction) in a Japanese company is actually much more democratic than one normally finds in Western companies, which is one of the reasons it is often difficult for foreigners to understand and work with it. In dealing with any Japanese group it helps to take the approach that you are dealing with a small, highly democratic, highly defensive, and very suspicious small country.

The strength of the faction system is that once a project or course of action is agreed upon—after it has been thoroughly studied and discussed—the whole group works together like a well-trained football team. The weakness of the system is that it is unable to respond quickly and tends to pull the caliber of the group well below the level of its most capable members.

Centuries of conditioning in group-think and in acting in groups instead of as individuals has resulted in the Japanese developing a highly refined ability to communicate with each other with what one might call "herd telepathy"—but what in Japan has far more colorful names.

6

Using the Art of the Belly

Non-verbal communication and intuition play a significant role in all personal relations in Japan, including all facets of business. This phenomenon is, of course, a direct outgrowth of a highly sophisticated and stylized culture that is over two thousand years old—a culture in which physical etiquette routinely took precedence over all other considerations.

As the centuries passed and the Japanese became more and more homogenized creatures of a monocultural society, packed into a tiny area, living in extended families, and working in consensus-controlled groups, verbal communication became superfluous in many of the common situations of life. To a remarkable degree, everybody thought very much alike, behaved in the same highly controlled manner, and reacted herd-like in virtually all situations.

While this degree of cultural conditioning certainly no longer exists in Japan, enough of it remains in the language, in the common education, common life, and work experiences that "communicating without talking" is still ranked high among the characteristic qualities the Japanese ascribe to themselves.

One area of "Japanese expertise" that plays a key role in business in Japan is known as *hara-gei* (hah-rah gay-e) or "the art of the belly." This refers to making decisions on the basis of gut feeling—a viscereal reaction to an individual or proposal or situation. Many older Japanese businessmen take great pride in depending on their belly instead of their head in operating their businesses.

What they are using to guide their approach to business is an accumulation of Japanese wisdom that goes back for centuries—their ability to "read" other people, to get their cooperation and help by intuitively knowing how to approach them, treat them, and react to them, and thus meld the Japanese into an effective work-group.

Many Japanese believe that it is the strength and

power that derives from the use of this "Japanese way" that has made Japan so economically successful in the world today. Of course, the Japanese art of the belly is generally effective only when the Japanese are dealing with other Japanese—and is the reason why the Japanese, without extensive international experience, feel very uncomfortable in dealing with foreigners. Not being able to "read" the bellies of foreigners they cannot anticipate their reactions. There is, therefore, a significant amount of constant tension between un-Westernized Japanese and Westerners—tension that disturbs them and tires them.

One of the many things foreign businessmen need to know in their dealings with Japanese is how to reduce this tension and make the Japanese feel less strained, less tense when they are together—in other words, to make their bellies feel good.

7

Communicating Heart-to-Heart in Japan

There is another method of communication in Japan that might be described as more refined or more sophisticated than *hara-gei,* the art of the belly, which also plays a key role in dealing with the Japanese. This second form of sending and receiving in Japan is known as *ishin denshin* (ee-sheen dane-sheen), which is often translated as "heart-to-heart communication" or "Japanese telepathy."

Basically, the only difference between *ishin denshin* and *hara-gei* is that the former refers to the head and the latter to the belly, although there is a stronger connotation of "feeling" in *hara-gei* while *ishin denshin* has more of an image of pure communication—that is nevertheless based on harmony between hearts and mutual compatibility on the lowest as well as the highest level.

This is another aspect of Japan that in the minds of the Japanese separates them from foreigners, and is perceived as both an asset and a handicap. They see it as an advantage when they are dealing with other Japanese, and therefore as one of the reasons why Japan is "superior" to other countries. It is of no value to them and becomes a frustration, however, when they are dealing with foreigners because foreigners are not tuned in on the same communication wavelength.

Japanese businessmen will frequently say it is difficult to deal with foreigners because they cannot communicate heart-to-heart with them, and that their goal is to learn English well enough and learn how foreigners do business well enough to establish an *ishin denshin* relationship.

Foreign businessmen, who often do not have sufficient motivation to learn the Japanese language and

Japan's business culture to the extent that they could tap into the telepathic wavelength of their Japanese counterparts, can overcome the handicap to some extent by letting the Japanese know they are aware of the "practice" and have their own version that they are endeavoring to make compatible with the Japanese.

You do need to learn some key Japanese words and phrases, a degree of Japanese protocol, and an appreciation of some things Japanese (such as Japanese food and singing in *karaoke* bars), to be very convincing in your claims about *ishin denshin*.

It will certainly impress a Japanese businessman if, on your second or third meeting, you make a point of saying you want to develop a relationship with him that will allow you to communicate heart-to-heart. Interestingly enough, most of the belly-to-belly and heart-to-heart communication in Japan takes place in the *mizu shobai* (me-zuu show-bye) or "water business," a very insightful euphemism for the nighttime entertainment trades, not the daytime business period. This means that the inexperienced foreigner has a better chance of being able to use the *ishin denshin* code quickly, since drinking and consorting with sexy women in a cabaret, geisha inn, or soapland (massage parlor), is a pretty universal language where men are concerned.

A word of advice, however. It is better to take a page out of the book of many Japanese and not get totally soused during cabaret outings. On numerous occasions I have been part of Japanese-foreign groups on the town when one or more of the foreign contingent got sick-drunk and on some occasions passed out, making any form of communication impossible—besides presenting a very negative impression.

Japanese hosts are often relentless in pressing drinks on their foreign guests during cabaret parties. It is essential that you stay well within your capacity by cutting back sharply after the first few rounds, just sipping the drinks and/or dumping them when nobody is looking, and feigning a degree of drunkenness that keeps you in step with the Japanese side.

If a key Japanese leans over and quickly gives you a briefing on the state of your business with him, you want to be able to clearly understand the message and make any appropriate response (even if that is nothing more than nodding your head and thanking him).

The importance of *hara-gei* and *ishin denshin* becomes very clear when you realize that what *is not said* is often more important than what is said, and just as often is the key that opens or locks the door to business. Mastering this form of "Japanese telepathy" is not something one can do quickly or easily. It requires complete immersion in the culture of contemporary Japan, including significant mastery of the language, along with a good grasp of the cultural history of Japan.

This aspect of communication in Japan is one of the primary barriers facing any outsider who attempts to do business with the Japanese, and is also why so many foreigners end up having to work through Japanese surrogates to get anything done in Japan.

8
Management by Intuition

Given the cultural conditioning that resulted in the Japanese often assigning more importance to emotion than to reason, it is not surprising that such things as *hara-gei* or the "art of the belly" and *ishin denshin* or "heart-to-heart communication" play a key role in Japanese management. But on the more refined levels of management in Japan one encounters the ultimate in "managing by intuition."

The Japanese word used to express the idea of managing by intuition is *kongen* (kone-gane), which means "root" or "source" in relation to the universe—which may sound like pretty heavy stuff to foreign businessmen who have MBAs instead of MBBs (Master of Business Buddhism).

Kongen refers to the energy-wisdom that, in Buddhist thought, fuels the universe. According to Buddhist belief, it is accessible to man through meditation, which allows one to tap into the stream of wisdom and energy and make use of it.

Japan's best-known proponent of *kongen* was the legendary Konosuke Matsushita, founder of the Matsushita Electric empire (National, Panasonic, etc.). Matsushita attributed his extraordinary success to regularly tapping into the intelligence of the universe, and decreed that all Matsushita managers spend a part of their work period tuned in to the universal mind.

While Matsushita was the most prominent modern-day practitioner of managing by intuitive intelligence, this concept is the key to the management success of *all* Japanese companies—although I am tempted to label it "Japanese cultural intelligence," since it appears inseparable from the Japanese mind-set and traditional social system.

During the 1950s and early 60s many Japanese companies made an attempt to convert their management system to American-style management. All the attempts failed, some of them with drastic results, forcing the companies to go back to the Japanese way. Few attempted to follow in Matsushita's footsteps, but what they were doing, regardless of how it was labeled, was following the traditional Japanese way of organizing and treating people, and getting an awful lot out of them in the process.

In any event, when the foreign businessman in Japan runs up against something he thinks doesn't make logical sense, he has probably had an encounter with *kongen*. If he is inspired to go out and buy himself a cushion to meditate on, he may learn something.

9

Pass the Zen, Please

I do not advocate that foreigners wanting to do business with the Japanese immediately run to a temple and sign up for a course in Zen. But I do suggest that familiarity with the concept and precepts of Zen would be of significant value in dealing with the intangible, esoteric, philosophical facets of the Japanese business system.

In Japan there is almost always a *tatemae* (facade) and a *honne* (the reality behind the facade). The universal facade that covers Japan like a blanket is its etiquette system. Other facades include such diverse things as cabarets in Japan's famous *mizu shobai* (mezuu show-bye), or "water trades," and the colorful kimono that women use as a "face" to present to the public. Looking at many aspects of Japan, one sees a surface that may hide any number of realities.

The same is true in business. What you see, and what the inexperienced foreigner is apt to take at face value, is often far from the truth. The surface harmony that prevails in most Japanese companies, for example, generally masks a morass of friction and discontent, as *wa* suffers more and more from the strains

34

of changing lifestyles and changing expectations.

Japanese society in general has traditionally been based on presenting a carefully fashioned face to the public and outside world, while taking great pains to camouflage reality behind manners, screens, their language, and other opaque barriers. The challenge is to discern what is real and what is facade, to see beyond the *tatemae* to the *honne,* and one of the skills that has traditionally helped the Japanese in seeing beyond their own illusions was derived from Zen.

The first stage of Zen, for all of its own *tatemae,* is nothing more than being able to distinguish between what appears to be real (or what we would like to be real) and reality itself. The second stage of Zen requires that a person develop the ability to eliminate his own self from the duality, from what he is and thinks he is to what exists outside of him, and, if he wants to go all the way, merge his being into the reality before him.

In the Japanese context of things, Zen was traditionally the vehicle by which people gained extraordinary skill in arts, crafts, and other pursuits. By physical discipline and meditation they first got their own selves under control. Then they learned how to discern the essence of what they saw before them, whether it was a rock, tree, metal sword, or human being. Then, by becoming one with the thing before them, they could use its essence in a natural way.

Probably the most notorious use of Zen was in the

training of swordsmen. After years of rigorous physical and mental training, the greatest swordsmen came close to becoming a part of their swords. Straining the analogy, their swords would therefore strike, perfectly, whatever blow they thought of because they and the sword were the same. The greatest of Japan's sword masters were virtually unbeatable during their peak years. This invincibility, of course, represents the Japanese ideal in all things, including business.

The lesson you can take from this facet of the Japanese way is to do your best to set aside your emotions and preconceived ideas in any meeting or relationship with a Japanese businessman, and to attempt to discern the reality behind the visible scenario. This is, of course, just another way of saying determine the facts, the cold, hard facts, before you commit yourself.

10

Putting Your Best Face Forward

In the Japanese context there is no neat separation between business and personal life. The larger the company the more apt it is to play a vital role in all the key areas of the lives of its employees—from housing and education to entertainment and recreation. The needs and concerns of the workplace often take precedence over personal affairs.

Larger Japanese companies do not hire to fill slots; they hire "recruits" who receive general orientation and then are assigned to departments where they receive ongoing on-the-job training. Those hired as white-collar workers, particularly managerial candidates, are regularly rotated among departments to give them a broad perspective of the company and its operation. Regular employment for males is presumed to be for life.

Japanese employers automatically expect total loyalty, total conformity to company policy and culture, and a dedication to work and the welfare of the company that transcends personal concerns.

Given this paternalistic approach to personnel management, Japanese companies give high priority to character and personality in their hiring practices. They also give substantial credence to the ranking of the schools potential employees attended, and to their family backgrounds. With some specific exceptions in technical areas, any previous work experience, special knowledge, or aggressive ambition an applicant might have may be considered a minus instead of a plus (because it could hinder his being molded into a company man).

Not surprisingly, when Japanese companies are approached by representatives of foreign companies they tend to use the same yardstick to evaluate foreign managers and employees that is used in their own firms. The evaluation begins with the perceived image of the individual company—whatever it is—and then jumps immediately to the representatives of that firm—their age, their title, how long they have been with the company, their educational background, any previous relationship with Japan, any personal Japanese contacts they may have, what they know about Japan, what their attitude is toward Japan, how they rank in their own company, and then moves on to why the foreign company chose to approach them (of all the other companies in Japan), who introduced them, and so on—all personal factors that the Japanese want to know before entering into serious discussions with anyone about anything.

The foreign businessman wanting to do business with the Japanese should anticipate this kind and degree of interest on the personal level, and do everything possible to present the most acceptable face. This means the foreign front man should be selected on the basis of criteria known to be acceptable—and generally speaking, the more impressive the better.

Here is a list of qualifications that are ideal for the foreign businessman who is going to be assigned to Japan (and are equally applicable to the foreign businessman visiting Japan in search of a Japanese partner or connection):

1) Since the man will have to deal with Japanese middle managers who are in their late 30s and 40s, he

should be in the same age range or above, but he should not be younger.

2) The man should have a calm, patient personality, and be able to think logically and rationally and express himself clearly. If he has well-honed intuitive powers, so much the better. He should be secure in his own knowledge and ability and persistent in working toward the company goals.

3) He should have the full confidence and trust of top management back home, and have both his responsibilities and authority clearly spelled out. If he does not have decision-making power, he should be guaranteed that when he asks for a decision from the head office it will be forthcoming in a matter of hours or days. Most foreign managers in Japan say they have as much trouble getting decisions out of their home offices as they do in dealing with the Japanese.

4) The more experience the man has already had with Japan and the more he knows about Japan, the better—if he is able to use this experience and knowledge in a non-threatening, cooperative way that reassures the Japanese rather than turns then off. This includes having an outgoing, likeable personality, and—this is very important—that he likes the Japanese well enough to enjoy their company. It helps if he is a modest drinker and likes a night out on the town (at least once a month).

5) At the same time, the man should not be naive or gullible, and should at all times insist on the

philosophy of fairness and the policy of reciprocity.

6) The man should have pride in his own country and not bad-mouth it to the Japanese. The Japanese are often critical of the U.S. and other foreign countries, but they have heard too much criticism by foreigners of their own countries—particularly Americans—and tend to regard such behavior as an attempt to curry favor with them. They may also take it as a sign that the individual is not a man of honor since he will not stand up for his own country. They often have a better understanding of both our weaknesses and strengths than we do, and they are very much aware that despite the faults of the American business system, for example, they still depend on the American economy for much of their prosperity.

11

Identifying Your Company

Large foreign companies going to Japan for the first time often mistakenly assume that their home-country reputation precedes them— that the Japanese know who they are, and are impressed. This is generally not the case at all. About the only foreign companies whose names are familiar to the Japanese are those that are doing business in

Japan and that have achieved a high degree of public recognition there. Just like most Americans and Europeans, the Japanese tend to ignore completely things that do not impact directly on their work or personal lives.

The awareness of foreign companies in Japan, including those on the scale of the *Fortune 500,* naturally tends to be limited to groups that have a professional interest in that particular industry, and even then, with a few exceptions, the awareness is shallow and it is unwise to leave it at that level.

This means that most companies wanting to establish a business relationship with a Japanese firm must start from the beginning. And while paid-in capital, share of the market, annual sales, profits, and other such numbers are important, the Japanese view is that people make the company. They want to know who the executives are. Before committing themselves to any kind of relationship, they have to get to know the foreign executives, to like and to trust them. They do not go into long-term relationships just on the basis of product and price.

Prior to approaching any Japanese company with any kind of proposal, the foreign firm, regardless of its size, should prepare historical and personal data on its top executives and any lower managers who will be involved with the project. The foreign company must also be prepared to go through a relatively long getting-acquainted period during which personal ties

41

are formed and cemented by various social and cultural means—and the potential Japanese partner checks you out through banks and other connections.

This vital step can be shortened considerably by bringing in third parties who are known to the Japanese side and who can in effect act as guarantors for the unknown foreign firm. This additional ingredient is even more effective when the third party has a business relationship with the Japanese partner you are approaching. More about this later.

Other helpful things when starting from scratch to develop a business relationship with a Japanese company include testimonial letters from political dignitaries (mayors, governors, high-level bureaucrats), scientists and educators with impressive titles and/or achievements, and chief executive officers of large companies whose names at least might be recognizable to the Japanese.

When visited by Japanese representatives of the company you are wooing you can also get substantial mileage out of arranging for them to meet (and have their pictures taken with) political dignitaries. The Japanese are also favorably impressed by meetings with well-known authors of business books that have presented Japan in a favorable light, but they are even more impressed by movie stars whose films are regularly shown in Japan.

When introducing your company it is unwise to exaggerate or paint a picture that will not stand up under scrutiny and the test of time. The main points to get across are sincerity, integrity, stability, creativity, and goodwill. The Japanese put great stock in all of these attributes, especially creativity. Their home market is so competitive and so conditioned to the regular appearance of new products that they have put creativity at the forefront of their marketing strategy. This ingredient alone is often enough to get their attention.

12

Knowing What You're Talking About

The number of foreign businessmen who go to Japan cold or make long-distance offers to Japanese companies without having made any effort to learn something about the Japanese market is incredible. Their ambitious programs are often based on nothing more substantial than news media reports they have heard or read.

In contrast to this, the Japanese are inveterate researchers and collectors of information. Japan's large trading companies have worldwide information-gathering networks that are not even approached in scale by foreign commercial companies, and are said to surpass the efficiency and effectiveness of such intelligence services as the U.S.'s CIA and the U.S.S.R.'s KGB.

Since the mid-1950s the Japanese have been swarming over the world on research trips. Even the smallest businessman who wants to do business abroad will take the time and spend the money to travel overseas, visiting retail outlets, wholesalers, and manufacturers in whatever product area interests him. And what is just as important, when they find something of interest and take it back to Japan they often improve on it. Just one example is a do-it-yourself supply store in Tokyo's Shibuya district, based on the American Handyman concept. The display innovations created by the store were startling, and it immediately struck me that American do-it-yourself store operators should come to Tokyo and see what has been done with their basic idea.

Knowing nothing or very little about the Japanese market is probably the biggest failing of most foreign companies wanting to do business in Japan, putting them at a serious disadvantage when they approach a Japanese company. The obvious solution to this problem is that a commitment must be made to spend the necessary money and time to find out what is going on in the Japanese market, how it works, and where a foreign company might fit in.

There are a number of options in how to go about researching an area of the Japanese market. Research companies in Japan can be retained. Staff can be sent to Japan. And there are dozens to hundreds of sources of market data in English. This data is available in published form on a daily, weekly, monthly, and annual basis, and can be purchased by anyone. The sources include various ministries and agencies of the Japanese government, trade associations, research institutes, marketing services, advertising agencies, insurance firms, securities companies, banks, data banks, etc.

Some of these publications are available on a subscription basis. Some are free. Others can be purchased individually, directly from the publishers, or from fulfillment centers. Two of the major suppliers of printed materials on Japan:

Government Publications Service Center
(GPSC)
(Seifu Kankobutsu Sabisu Senta)
1–2–1 Kasumigaseki, Chiyoda-ku
Tokyo, Japan 100

GPSC is sales agent for numerous government and private commercial publications on Japan. An annual catalog is available, and mail orders are accepted. Among just Ministry of Finance publications available from the GPSC: *Annual Report on Business Cycle Indicators; Indicators of Science and Technology; Japanese Economic Indicators; An Outline of Japanese Taxes; Polls on Preferences in National Life;* and *Quality of the Environment in Japan.*

Intercontinental Marketing Corporation (IMC)
CPO Box 971, Tokyo, Japan 100–91

IMC is sales agent for most of Japan's English-language publishers. Annual catalogs include *Japan English Books in Print* and *Japan English Magazine Directory*. This directory covers periodicals of all kinds. The IMC handles subscriptions and individual sales on a worldwide basis.

Other sources of information on Japan:

> American Chamber of Commerce in Japan
> (Zainichi Beikoku Shoko Kaigi Sho)
> Fukide Bldg., No. 2, 7th Floor
> 4–1–21 Toranomon, Minato-ku
> Tokyo, Japan 105

Chamber of Commerce publications include: *The Journal of the American Chamber of Commerce in Japan* and *Living in Japan*.

> Business Intercommunications Inc.
> Noguchi Bldg.
> CPO Box 587
> 3–13–3 Kita Aoyama, Minato-ku,
> Tokyo, Japan 107

Publications include: *Directory of Foreign Capital Affiliated Firms in Japan; A Wage Survey of Foreign Capital Affiliated Firms in Japan;* and the *White Paper on the Japanese Economy.*

> Japan External Trade Organization (JETRO)
> (Nihon Boeki Shinko Kai)

JETRO Bldg.
2-2-5 Toranomon, Minato-ku
Tokyo, Japan 105

JETRO publications include: *Access to Japan's Import Market; China Newsletter; Exporting to Japan; Facts and Finds Series; Focus Japan; Japan Industrial & Technological Bulletin; JETRO Marketing Series; Keys to Success in the Japanese Market (1980–84); Update; White Paper on International Trade;* and *Your Market in Japan.*

JETRO's network of offices abroad, where its publications are generally available, are known as Japan Trade Centers. At present there are branches in New York, Chicago, Houston, Los Angeles, San Francisco, in the U.S.; Toronto, Edmonton, Montreal, Vancouver, in Canada; Paris, London, and Hamburg, in Europe.

Japan Statistical Association
(Nihon Tokei Kyokai)
95 Wakamatsu-cho, Shinjuku-ku
Tokyo, Japan 162

Publications include: *Annual Report on the Consumer Price Index; Annual Report on the Family Income and Expenditure Survey; Annual Report on Labor Force Survey; Annual Report on Retail Price Survey; Annual Report on Unincorporated Enterprise Survey; Employment Status Survey; Establishment Census of Japan; Family Saving Survey; Housing Survey of Japan;* and the *Japan Statistical Yearbook.*

Japan Tariff Association
(Nihon Kanzei Kyokai)
Jibiki Building No. 2
4–7–8 Kojimachi, Chiyoda-ku
Tokyo, Japan 102

Publications include: *Customs Tariff Schedules of Japan; Export Statistical Schedule; Import Statistical Schedule; Japan Exports and Imports* (commodity by country); *Japan Exports and Imports* (country by commodity); *Japan Laws and Regulations Concerning Customs, Duties, and Customs Procedures;* and *Summary Report: Trade of Japan.*

For a more comprehensive list of sources for English-language business-related information on Japan, see *Things Japanese: The Whole Japan Book* (Lincolnwood, Illinois: Passport Books/NTC Publishing Group).

Well-informed and well-connected consultants on doing business in Japan are also available in most countries, and particularly in the U.S. These include private individuals, consulting firms, law firms, and accounting firms. These sources are generally known to Japan society chapters, world trade associations, and the international banking communities—and in the U.S. to the American Graduate School of International Management in Glendale, Arizona.

Note: There is also a list of support organizations and consultants for the Japanese market available from the U.S. Department of Commerce for a small fee.

13

Coming Up with the Right Bait

Foreign businessmen who have not done business with Japan before and know very little about the country tend to be naive and simplistic in their opinions about what product or service might succeed in the Japanese market, or what kind of overseas investment the Japanese will be interested in. Those who are in this category will often start out with the premise that they will be able to sell to a certain percentage of the population, and all of their dreams flow from this fantasy. Or they assume, from reports in the news media, that since Japan is in an "investment frenzy" they can get a piece of the action just by announcing that they have something for sale.

This attitude and behavior ignores a world of reality, beginning with the basics of Japanese thinking and how their business system works, including the highly advanced stage of the Japanese economy with its intense competition. It particularly ignores the sophisticated, comprehensive, and intense way the Japanese investigate investment opportunities—a process that can take anywhere from a year to five years.

The foreign company wanting to do business with the Japanese must take an equally long-term view and prepare meticulously for the first encounter. As we have already discussed, two primary keys to establishing dialogue with a Japanese company are a thorough introduction of your own firm and an equally thorough introduction of its top people. Presuming the Japanese are attracted or impressed, this is just the first stage of the relationship.

The next key is what you are offering the Japanese. Obviously, it has to be something that has merit in their eyes, that fits into their operation and goals, and has a high probability of success. The attraction must be strong enough that it will take precedence over anywhere from dozens to hundreds of other projects that are available to the company. It must possess numerous attributes to qualify for serious consideration, and really have significant potential to win out over the company's other options.

Regardless of the product, service or investment, being able to judge its suitability for the Japanese market requires a considerable amount of experience and expertise—or a shot-in-the-dark kind of luck.

The point is, rather than take potshots in the dark—it is better to do some homework first. The one thing that stands out in any survey of foreign firms that have succeeded in doing business with the Japanese is that they learned how to use the Japanese system.

The old saying, find a need (or a want) and fill it, applies just as much in Japan as anywhere else. The challenge is to come up with products or investment opportunities that meet this criterion.

14

Focusing on the Right Connection

Once you have determined what product or service or investment opportunity you are going to offer to the Japanese market, the next challenge is to identify and qualify the most likely prospects for your Japanese connection, whether it is to be an agent, partner, importer, distributor, or investor.

There are numerous factors that must be considered: your company size and experience; the nature of the product or investment opportunity; the uniqueness factor; competition; and so on. In the case of products and services to be sold in Japan the factors having to do with the exclusive group alignment of business, the tendency for large Japanese companies to be vertically as well as horizontally integrated, the multi-layered nature of the traditional distribution system, the monopolistic tendencies of the large *sogo shosha* (soe-go show-shah) trading companies, the control exercised by the various ministries over foreign imports (especially the role of the Ministry of Health and Welfare in food imports), are just some of the considerations.

Approaching one of the large trading companies, with their overseas offices and bilingual staff, may appear to be the obvious choice. After all, they are experts in many fields of marketing in Japan; they have extraordinary financial as well as political clout; they have a high image and give a new foreign client instant credibility in the Japanese marketplace, etc.

The downside of going with a large trading company (if they will have you) can be devastating in the long run. Your account becomes one of thousands competing for the attention of qualified managers, and often with similar products also handled by the trading company. If your project is not high priority, it does not get the best people or the most resources, and can easily get stuck in the system.

All of the large trading companies are aligned with specific groups of other companies in banking, manufacturing, distributing, and retailing. Each group has its own "territory" that is vertically structured from top to bottom—from obtaining raw materials to retailing finished products to consumers. In many areas and ways, these groups are exclusive and inclusive and therefore limiting. If you are in the Mitsubishi group, for example, your product may be handled only by other companies affiliated with the same group.

Because of this uniquely Japanese system, there are often occasions when it is better to go with a non-aligned company that can cross "group" borders and can also give a higher priority to your project because it is more important to the firm. A number of recent foreign successes in Japan have been with small, unknown entrepreneurial companies founded and operated by exceptionally capable, energetic individuals who overcame all obstacles with the power of their personalities, ideas, and hard work.

The success rate of foreign companies forging tie-ups with Japanese companies is surprisingly low, however, and should serve as a warning to companies contemplating doing business in Japan. The reasons for the low batting average are invariably the same—the foreign company took the fast, easy way out and signed up without really knowing what they were getting into.

It is, in fact, very difficult for a foreign company not intimately familiar with Japan to make a sound decision about a potential Japanese connection. There are so many factors and variables, many of them subtle and invisible, that should be taken into consideration. While it is possible to find out a great deal about a company in just a few days of investigation, both its strengths and its weaknesses, it is still difficult for a company without extensive experience in Japan to make the best choice for a long-term relationship. You could start out, however, by obtaining copies of the

Japan Company Handbook, published by Toyo Keizai Shinposha, and *Industrial Groupings in Japan,* published by Dodwell Marketing Consultants. Both directories are usually available at stores that specialize in books on Japan, such as the Kinokuniya chain.

Often the most practical recourse open to the foreign company, regardless of its size, is to enlist the aid of third parties in Japan—bankers, accountants, government officials, advertising agencies, market research firms, consultants, and lawyers as well as people in the business category concerned—to advise them. There is a tendency for foreign businessmen to accept what they see and hear in Japan at face value, often to their later chagrin. Reality in Japan is often not what the foreigner perceives it to be.

Both Japanese and foreigners often make decisions on the basis of "gut feelings"—in fact, this is a significant aspect of the Japanese way of doing business—but problems arise when these decisions are cross-cultural. The gut feelings a foreigner gets from a Japanese situation are much more likely to be wrong than right. It is generally much safer to go with the professional advice of a third party than to rely on feelings.

Of course, there are exceptions, such as when you are dealing with an entrepreneurial type whose character and personality tip the odds in his favor, or with the founder-owner of a so-called "one-man company," who calls all of the shots, and makes a strong personal commitment to you and your project.

15

Finding the Right Connection

Finding and making Japan connections may not be as difficult as it first appears, even for novice newcomers. Obvious contact points include Japanese embassies and consulates abroad. Their information is invariably dated but they can provide names and addresses of other more current sources of information. The commerce departments or ministries (and regional field offices) of respective countries are also sources for general information on doing business in Japan, including very pertinent data on the laws, regulations, and procedures for importing and exporting.

The next obvious contact points are the appropriate embassies and consulates maintained by foreign countries in Japan. The Tokyo embassies of all the leading nations have very active commercial sections dedicated to helping their businessmen succeed in Japan. The larger embassies, in particular the American, British, German, French, Canadian, and Australian embassies, are especially active in the commercial area, providing numerous business services to their nationals.

The American Embassy in Tokyo operates a Business Information Center that offers various services to U.S. businessmen, from advice on who to contact and help in setting up appointments to assistance in negotiating with private companies as well as government agencies. The *Japan Market Information Report,* published by the Center, can be very valuable in keeping up with what is going on in the Japanese market. The Center also maintains a large library of information about Japanese companies. The address:

> Business Information Center
> Embassy of the United States of America
> 1-10-5 Akasaka, Minato-ku
> Tokyo, Japan 107
> Tel. (03) 224-5075

Next in line and closer still to the action are the foreign chambers of commerce in Tokyo. The American Chamber of Commerce in Japan (ACCJ) is one of the most active, with several on-going research and service committees designed to provide members with up-to-date information about every important aspect of doing business in Japan, from market research, advertising, and distribution to taxes, housing, and schools for expatriate kids. The chamber conducts regular "business breakfasts" for its members and guests, featuring speakers and panelists who are expert in various aspects of Japan's business world.

Any businessman can join the American Chamber of Commerce in Japan (membership is not limited to Americans). There is a non-resident membership for businessmen who live abroad and want the advantage of receiving the chamber's various publications, and utilizing its office on visits to Japan. Becoming a member of the chamber plugs you into one of the largest and most effective foreign-oriented networks in Japan. For more information, contact the chamber at (03) 433-5381. (The address is on page 46.)

Other prime contact points are the various service clubs that are active and popular in Japan. Probably the two largest and most important are the Rotary Club and the Kiwanis Club. The Japanese take membership in these clubs very seriously, and also look at them as contact points for their own international relations. Foreign members of these clubs can invariably tap into the Japanese membership and take advantage of a wide network of contacts. See the *Japan Yellow Pages* for current numbers and addresses.

Sister-city relationships are another good contact point for beginning to establish a Japanese network. Some of the more aggressive cities around the world have sister-city relations with as many as a dozen Japanese cities, from Kagoshima at the southern tip of Kyushu to Sapporo on the northern island of Hokkaido.

Professional associations are another avenue for getting inside the outer moat of Japan. There is an association for virtually every endeavor—cultural, social, educational, scientific, economic, etc. Letters and visits to the appropriate office will invariably provide you with contacts.

On the business side, foreign as well as Japanese banks are key contact points, and are often all you need to get started. The foreign branches of Japanese banks can be especially helpful, as can the branches of foreign banks in Japan. The larger Japanese trading companies have offices all over the world, and can often provide points of entry into the Japanese business community.

Local chapters of Japan societies are also primary sources about local Japanese activity as well as Japanese contacts. In the U.S., the Japan Society (333 E. 47th St., New York, N.Y. 10017) has more than a dozen chapters around the country.

There are a number of annual English-language directories available in hotel bookshops in Japan, as well as in many outlets abroad, that provide the names and addresses of all the entities mentioned above, plus hundreds more.

These publications include the *Japan Yellow Pages* and directories of the foreign subsidiaries and branches of Japanese companies around the world, including the *Directory of Offices and Affiliates of Japanese Companies in the U.S. and Canada*. There are also *Japan Yellow Pages* published in Los Angeles and in New York covering those areas.

16

Putting Your Life on the Line

One of the qualities that Japanese most often find lacking in foreign companies desiring to do business in Japan is that of commitment. They point out repeatedly, and rightly so, that anyone who wants to succeed in Japan—whether Japanese or foreign—must make a firm long-term commitment. Many foreign companies that have come to Japan have given up before getting started or withdrawn at the first serious setback.

There are a dozen or more aspects to the Japanese rationale. First, it simply takes longer to get things started in Japan than it does in such freewheeling economies as the U.S. and Canada. The reasons for this range from the cold molasses pace of the bureaucracy to the need to establish a supporting network of personal relationships over a period of time. Another reason is that business itself is done in a much more personal way, requiring a much larger investment in time to make and maintain contacts.

Business relationships are not based solely on products and profits. Even more important is the confidence, trust, and loyalty that is the hallmark of the

Japanese system, and something that requires years and a lot of investment to develop.

The Japanese are acutely aware that their business system is extremely difficult for foreigners to master and that the Japanese cultural environment in general constitutes a major obstacle to a foreign company coming to and succeeding in Japan. They agree on the one hand that the system itself is at fault and should be changed, but on the other hand they note that they also have to operate within the system, and if they can do it, foreigners who really try should also be able to do it.

As the Japanese have become more successful and self-assertive they have become more critical of both the commitment and the ability of foreign companies wanting to penetrate the Japanese market. This does not make it easier for the foreign company, since there is a degree of built-in prejudice from the beginning and a tendency for the Japanese to maintain the present system because it works well for them and acts as an unofficial barrier to keep foreign companies at bay.

The official Japanese stance of favoring the entry of more foreign companies into Japan can be a key to making it happen, once the foreign businessman has made the necessary commitment. The foreign businessman, as one of his first moves, should systematically solicit the cooperation and support of as many Japanese government offices and agencies as possible, openly and frankly asking for their help.

Your early contacts, including the commercial department of your embassy in Tokyo, can advise you on the government entities whose advice and endorsement would benefit you.

17

Avoiding the Second-Class Pitfall

The Japanese obsession with quality has a broad impact that influences all areas and levels of life and work in the country. The Japanese image of most foreign products as being inferior to their own—whether the image is right or wrong—is well recognized as a major problem for its foreign trading partners. This facet of Japanese culture is of immediate concern to the foreign company wanting to do business with Japan for the first time because it may prevent the company from even getting onto the playing field.

The first impression the Japanese have of a foreign company is often drawn from its stationery, brochures, annual reports, and (maybe) catalogs. The impression imparted by these printed materials goes a long way toward setting the foreign company's image in their minds. If the materials are not well designed and well printed on attractive paper stock, the image is negative and immediately gives the impression that the company is not professional, not sophisticated, not successful, and not concerned about its image.

Foreign companies approaching Japan often begin with two strikes against them because they go in with second- or third-class printed materials—because they are less concerned about the quality of the materials and see no reason for spending the kind of money necessary to get first-class or superior design and printing. Besides doing without professional design, too many foreign companies also stint on printing by going to small, cheap, neighborhood job shops for their work.

Unless the foreign company is large and well-known in Japan (in which case it may be able to successfully flout local standards), it is strongly advised that all materials to be used in any presentation or promotion be specially designed and printed with Japanese quality standards in mind. As it happens, the Japanese are particularly sensitive to design and printing and automatically make comparisons between Japanese printing and foreign printing. Not surprisingly, they believe their printing and design industries are the best in the world.

Going in with second- or third-class printing reinforces the Japanese belief that foreign businessmen are basically not concerned about quality, and this reflects badly on foreign businessmen in other important areas as well.

18
Going in Alone

More and more foreign companies entering Japan are side-stepping the problems of finding, qualifying, and tying-up with Japanese agents or partners by going in on their own, making their own distribution contacts or establishing their own systems. While this approach presents a different set of factors, it obviously works for some kinds of operations.

Probably the strongest reason for deciding to go it alone in Japan is a desire to avoid the hidebound, multi-leveled distribution system, with its age-old loyalties and stranglehold on both manufacturers and retailers. Other obvious factors are maintaining more control over their operation and reaping more of the rewards, including the value that comes from learning how to market in Japan directly.

As the consumer economy has matured and the number and variety of new retail chain stores without long ties to wholesalers has mushroomed, it has offered more opportunities for direct distribution by both Japanese and foreign companies. Direct-mail marketing had also become a major industry in Japan by 1989 and is growing at an impressive annual rate.

The key to successful direct distribution in the retail trade as well as direct-marketing to consumers in Japan is hiring highly qualified Japanese managers, and in having the persistence to develop the necessary relationships, awareness, and trust.

This means that a great deal of your initial effort must be spent in identifying exceptionally qualified people and then making them an offer they cannot refuse. There are several management recruiting agencies in Tokyo that specialize in this area. Those with a high success rate include the Cambridge Corporation and Helpmates International.

The Cambridge Corporation
No. 3 Kowa Bldg.
1-11-45 Akasaka, Minato-ku
Tokyo, Japan 107

19

Men with Fighting Spirit

Not surprisingly, the Japanese have a special word to describe the qualities that are ideal in a businessman, especially one who is to be entrusted to launch a new project or new product. This term, *konjo* (kone-joe), means "nature" or "spirit," and in this context means "fighting spirit."

The origin of *konjo* no doubt goes back to the days (actually not so long ago) of the samurai, Japan's feudalistic warrior class, whose training included not only mastering an array of martial arts but also mastering and steeling the spirit—to the point that they could slit open their bellies in a formalized suicide ritual when the occasion called for it.

It is still common in Japan to think of business strategy and tactics in military terms (the books of Chinese and Japanese military stategists have long been required reading for those aspiring to careers in management). A *konjo ga aru otoko* (kone-joe gah ah-rue oh-toe-koe) or "man with fighting spirit," the type of manager who will go after his goals with all the dedicated planning and ferocity of a warrior about to attack a well-entrenched enemy, knowing there will be no quarter given and no retreat, remains the standard by which all others are measured.

The foreign company looking for a representative or a top employee in Japan, especially one that is to head up a marketing operation, would be well-advised to add *konjo* to the list of qualifications for such an individual. Just using the term to your contacts and any recruiters you might use will immediately clarify what kind of person you are looking for and the way you intend to approach the market.

20

Rules of Employment

If you are contemplating establishing your own company in Japan, it is essential to keep in mind that labor laws in Japan are comprehensive and precise. It is critical that foreign companies setting up an operation in Japan obtain local expert assistance in providing not only the right legal framework for their operations but also an effective cultural environment for their employees.

There is a strong tendency for foreign businessmen to inject some of the laws and customs of their own country into their rules of employment for their Japanese staff. This almost never works well, except perhaps in an office with only two or three people, and each additional staff member increases the likelihood that it will not work at all.

As much as they might like the sound of the American or European way of management, and as often as they might say they prefer it and want it when being considered for employment by a foreign firm, non-Westernized Japanese invariably find that it does not suit either their emotional needs or their concept of what is fair.

Foreign companies that are persuaded by the Japanese employees, or insist on their own in utilizing Western management practices, almost always find themselves in trouble within a short period of time.

Once the Japanese style *shumu kisoku* (shuu-muu kee-soe-kuu) or work rules are in place—and signed by every Japanese employee—you can add some personal or Western flavor to your management style if you find it effective, but the protection of having precedent- and court-sanctioned work rules is essential.

21

Going in with a Japanese Connection

If you opt to go into Japan through a Japanese connection, your primary challenge will be to develop and maintain a working relationship with the Japanese side that is close enough and effective enough to protect your interests and allow you to make a contribution to the project. This is not as easy as it might first appear. Because of the nature of the business environment and the Japanese way of doing things, you have put the future of the project in Japanese hands.

As soon as the agreement is signed, chances are that both your goals and your ideas about how to achieve them will begin to diverge. The Japanese side will naturally take the position that they know more about how to do things in Japan than you do, and will often proceed without explaining or informing you of their moves. No matter how strong your position is on paper, the Japanese side will be the one that implements the project and sets its tenor and tone.

It is therefore very important that you come to a full, long-range understanding of mutual goals prior to signing any agreement, and that checks and balances that empower you to influence the broad scope of the program be written into the agreement.

As always, another important thing here is to have your own man in Japan—Japanese or foreign—who has the experience and knowledge to effectively interface between you and the Japanese side, and whom you can trust completely.

Whether in joint ventures or wholly owned foreign companies, there is invariably a natural division between the foreign staff and the Japanese staff, and there is often competition for power among the Japanese staff, which, whether intended or not, tends to isolate the foreign personnel.

In wholly owned foreign firms in Japan that have foreign CEOs there is a strong tendency for the Japanese side to assume that eventually the foreign CEO will be replaced by a Japanese CEO. The rationale is that, after all, the company is in Japan, so a Japanese CEO can naturally do a better job.

This attitude tends to set up a great deal of competitive tension within these companies, often with one or more of the more powerful Japanese executives constantly maneuvering to enhance their positions and to isolate the foreign CEO. In such cases, the foreign CEO often ends up having only some of the female employees and his own secretary on his side.

Generally speaking, some of the female employees will almost always side with the foreign staff because they perceive that the foreigners treat them with more respect, and give them more opportunities to advance.

Of course, the upside of going in with a Japanese connection is that the Japanese side does know how to operate in Japan, does have connections, and if sincere, aggressive, and capable, can make a significant contribution to the success of the project. By the same token, the foreign company going through a Japanese connection virtually forfeits the opportunity to learn how to do business in Japan on its own.

22

The Importance of Going to Japan

The Japanese knew in the 1950s and 60s that the ultimate key to learning about foreign markets and doing business abroad was to travel overseas to actually see the markets and experience dealing with their foreign counterparts on their home ground. This is a lesson that foreign businessmen wanting to do business with Japan must also learn.

Reading books and listening to others talk about working with the Japanese is a good beginning that can save a lot of time, expense, and frustration, but not going any further is like reading a romance novel without ever experiencing romance or studying a guide to riding a bicycle and never getting on a bike. It is a one-dimensional exercise that is far from the real thing.

To really grasp how the Japanese do business and how to deal with them effectively you have to take your clothes off and jump into the water; you have to feel and taste the nuances of their attitudes and behavior; you have to physically absorb the system into your body.

To do this even to a minor degree, you must go to Japan and personally experience it, physically and emotionally as well as intellectually. This means that once you are in Japan you have to get out of the international hotels and office buildings and spend time in department stores, on shopping streets, in restaurants, bars and cabarets, in major transportation terminals, on trains and subways, in schools, and if you can arrange it, in the homes of ordinary people.

This is the kind of investment involving time and

money that the average foreign businessman is all too often reluctant to make, and is one of the reasons why more foreign companies are not in the Japanese market. Ultimately, it could be one of the reasons why foreign businessmen lose even more of their own home markets to Japanese who are more aggressive, more determined, and work harder.

Ideally, the foreign company wanting to do business in Japan would do what the Japanese do when they want to penetrate a foreign market—send one or more of their best men there, for as much as a year or more, to do nothing but study the country, the people, the market, and how the business system works, developing cultural insights and skills that will help them live and work in the society.

23

Greasing the Skids

Regardless of the kind of project or nature of any business in which one proposes to become involved with an individual Japanese or a Japanese company, one of the key elements in establishing a relationship is to go in with a *shokaijo* (show-kie-joe), or introduction, from someone or some company of sufficient stature to get you across the moat, through the walls, and into the presence of a top executive.

Being group-oriented, with extraordinarily heavy obligations to their families, relatives, school friends, employers, and the government, the Japanese have traditionally avoided casual contact with strangers that might develop into more obligation, competition, or a conflict of interest with outside groups. Also, being conditioned to avoid individual responsibility, the Japanese have always been reluctant to take any kind of personal initiative on behalf of someone they do not know.

Traditional protocol made it mandatory that the only acceptable way the Japanese could develop a new relationship was if the person concerned was introduced to them by a mutual friend or third party with whom they had an established, positive relationship.

In the 1950s and 60s foreign businessmen often ignored this protocol in their business activities in Japan, either out of ignorance or arrogance. Foreigners regularly went to Japanese companies without appointments, and were almost always welcomed courteously, often by the highest-ranking individual in the office or company at that time. This special catering to foreigners diminished significantly in the 1970s, and is now rare, especially in larger firms.

While the historical sanctions enforcing *shokaijo* protocol have weakened considerably, it is still an expected and important facet of Japanese behavior. Generally speaking, Japanese companies will not respond to any approach made by people or companies they do not know, unless the approach is through an acceptable introduction. Self-introductions by phone or letter, which are perfectly acceptable in many Western countries, usually do not work in Japan.

Acceptable introductions on a personal level include those from friends or relatives, former professors or benefactors. On a company level, acceptable introductions to specific individuals include personal as well as established business connections, such as managers or executives of banks, other companies, associations, and government agencies.

The power or effectiveness of an introduction is, of course, determined by a number of factors. On a company level, an introduction by the department head of Mitsui Trading Company or the Bank of Tokyo is obviously going to carry more weight than one from a small, relatively unimportant enterprise. Likewise, an introduction by a well-known professor of a high-ranking university can gain you quick access to an otherwise unapproachable person.

When a Japanese wants to meet someone new, on a personal or business level, the first thing he does is review his list of contacts to see if he knows anyone who has a relationship with the individual or company he wants to call on, and who can provide him with an introduction. In earlier years, such introductions almost always involved physically taking the mutual contact's name card to the meeting and presenting it to the third party. Nowadays, it is usually sufficient to just make verbal reference to the go-between, generally by phone when calling in to set up an appointment or in a letter, if making contact from abroad.

Foreign businessmen in Japan are no longer automatically excused from following established custom, and in this case are strongly advised to take advantage of the customary etiquette for very practical reasons—it means the drawbridge will be let down, allowing you to cross the outer moat surrounding the company and state your case as an honorary insider instead of trying to communicate from the outside as a stranger.

As part of your research to identify the company you want to approach, and the individuals within the company that would be the most appropriate for you to talk to, you should also identify people who can provide you with introductions to them—preferably business contacts that are important to them, but personal contacts are also acceptable as a second choice. The ideal situation is to have an introduction to someone at the director level, and then, through him, move down to the department-head level and from there to the appropriate section or sections, where the work actually takes place. If you first approach a low-level employee, however, you may never gain access to management personnel.

24

Getting Help from Experts

Cultural arrogance and lack of cross-cultural experience often results in foreign businessmen automatically presuming they can establish themselves in Japan or with foreign-based Japanese companies without any outside help. Most cannot, and many of those who do eventually succeed could have saved themselves a lot of time, frustration, and money by enlisting the aid of *sodanyaku* (soe-dahn-yah-kuu) consultants or *chukai-sha* (chuu-kie-shah) go-betweens whose specialty is bridging the foreign-Japanese cultural and communication gaps.

The personal nature of business in Japan, the role of long-term connections in getting in to see the right people and getting things done, the subtle nuances of business relationships, and the protocol and maze of the Japanese system is not something that can be picked up overnight. Conventional wisdom, as learned by businessmen who have been stationed in Japan for a long time, is that it takes about three years minimum of on-the-job experience to become fairly efficient in operating with and within the Japanese system.

Most foreign companies setting up operations in Japan depend on their new Japanese employees to act as their advisors, go-betweens, and buffers in dealing with the Japanese bureaucracy and marketplace. Some are fortunate enough to find and employ very capable Japanese employees who can bridge the gap for them. This kind of serendipity is rare, however, and companies that are not so fortunate generally have a difficult and expensive time.

Foreign companies seeking to establish relationships and deal with Japanese companies from abroad may face fewer problems directly, but if they do not have in-house expertise (that is genuine), their chances of consummating a relationship—which they themselves initiated—with a Japanese company are minimal.

The recommended solution is an obvious one that is all too often ignored—obtaining the services of an experienced consultant and/or go-between. I distinguish between the two because a consultant is often involved only on the sidelines, giving advice and helping to develop strategy and tactics, while the *chukai-sha* or go-between gets down into the trenches, meets the other side face-to-face, and represents the interests of his client. Most go-betweens are usually qualified to act as consultants as well, but many consultants are not qualified to be go-betweens.

There are several classes and levels of consultants, ranging from Caucasian foreigners whose primary credentials are academic—they've read a lot of books and maybe done some fieldwork—to those who have lived and worked in Japan. A few of the latter speak Japanese well enough to conduct business in the language. There are also foreign consultants of Japanese ancestry who have first-hand experience and are fluent in the language, as well as Japanese consultants who are well-versed in English, and primarily service foreign clients.

Because of the sensitive nature of dealing with Japanese companies, and the extraordinary amount of knowledge and experience necessary for doing it effectively, most of the best *chukai-sha* or go-betweens are Japanese who have become at least semi-bilingual and bicultural and are able to function in both environments.

There are a limited number of non-Japanese offering their services as consultants on doing business with the Japanese who in fact are qualified to serve as go-betweens as well, and perform both functions. A significant percentage of these are of Japanese ancestry. As a general guideline, any go-between, whether Japanese or non-Japanese, should have spent at least 10 years in Japan working in and/or with Japanese companies on a daily basis, with a broad scope of experience.

It should be emphasized that virtually all problems that arise between Japanese and foreign companies begin and end with communication failures, not only in the sense of language but in cultural communication as well. It is therefore essential that any go-between you retain be thoroughly experienced in all aspects of the language and the business culture.

In the case of a go-between, the higher the stature of the individual the better. The ideal *chukai-sha* is a successful ex-businessman or high government official, at least in his late 40s (and often the older the better, since he will be dealing with men in this age bracket and above), whose background and connections are impressive enough that he is automatically afforded a high degree of respect.

Probably the best sources for lists of recommended consultants and go-betweens are the various foreign chambers of commerce in Japan.

25
Borrowing Face from Advisors

Another tried and proven technique for success in dealing with the Japanese for any purpose on any level is making use of "advisors." In fact, this is a practice that goes way beyond surface indications. It is an institution sanctified by the ages, and incorporates the Japanese philosophy of venerating and taking care of the elderly—with very practical applications.

When high company executives or government bureaucrats retire it is common for them to be appointed advisors to their former organizations, usually for life. It is also common for them to become advisors to other companies or organizations. This means not only that they will continue to have income, but also that the connections and experience they accumulated over a lifetime continue to be used, and the "face" they have in their industry does not go to waste.

Virtually every Japanese organization, including those of very modest size, has its advisors. Larger companies and organizations also retain professors and scientists who are still active in their fields along with those who have retired.

One of the first things the Japanese are likely to do in setting up a new enterprise is add a list of advisors to their roster. Many government and cultural organizations will have from three or four to twenty or more advisors. In academic and cultural circles especially, but in some political and commercial operations as well, these lists of advisors are often just window dressing, added to give legitimacy and image to the organization. In such cases, which are abundant, the advisors are seldom called on to give any advice, but they are invited to receptions and other events where their presence is an asset. Of course, they are paid fees for lending their names to such enterprises.

The benefit that a well-known advisor can bring to a company in Japan should not be underestimated, however, even when he actually gives little or no advice. In these cases it is his "face" that is being used. But there are just as many advisors who do in fact play active roles in the companies that retain them, not only giving advice but also opening doors and making connections.

The foreign company wanting to do business with Japan, whether in Japan or abroad, will invariably find that a highly respected advisor (or advisors) can make the road much smoother and shorter. I recommend that any company contemplating going into Japan put finding one suitable advisor (or more) on the top of the list of things to do. Companies already in Japan that do not have advisors, and believe they could or should be doing better, might be able to make a breakthrough with the help of a prestigious individual in their area of business.

26

Inviting the Japanese to Visit You

If you are the one who makes the first contact with a Japanese firm, and subsequently visits them in Japan as part of your presentation, it is good psychology and often good business to invite them to visit you in your office for a continuation of the dialogue or negotiations. The more important the project and the more interested the Japanese side, obviously the more likely they are to accept the invitation.

I make a point of this here because smaller foreign companies often fail to take advantage of getting the Japanese to come to them on their home ground; oftentimes because they are small and are afraid the Japanese side would not be sufficiently impressed. This is usually not a good excuse, because your size and everything else about you is most likely going to come out anyway, especially if you are the one who approached the Japanese company, since they are usually very meticulous in checking out potential suppliers or partners.

If you can get the Japanese to come to you, you have a number of home-ground advantages. They will automatically fall into the "dealing-with-foreigners-outside-of-Japan" mode, meaning you can follow your own native protocol in dealing with them in your overall approach, and just cater to their Japaneseness on the personal side—such as taking them to a good Japanese or Chinese restaurant if they have been outside of Japan for several days (by which time they will have begun to crave a familiar meal), and giving them a gift when they leave.

It also obviously gives you an opportunity to thoroughly acquaint them with your operation from the ground up, significantly reducing the amount of time it would otherwise normally take to establish the relationship you want with them. Of course, if they are not impressed enough with your company to continue pursuing the project, that is another matter. In any event, being frank and forthright in representing yourself and your company is the best policy. Companies that misrepresent themselves to the Japanese invariably get caught.

The Japanese will not normally expect a smaller company to pick up the tab for their travel or hotel accommodations if you invite them to visit you, especially if they are members of a larger company and you do not yet have a business relationship. It is good etiquette, however, to pay all restaurant bills when you dine with them except when the visitors make a point of inviting you—usually on their last night in town. The Japanese themselves are exceptionally generous about paying restaurant and other miscellaneous expenses of foreign guests, often saying things like "You are in Japan. You are our guest."

Interestingly, the Japanese generally do not expect the same degree of generosity from foreigners whom they visit abroad. The apparent reason for this attitude is that the Japanese have traditionally had a reputation of being big spenders when it came to entertaining and taking care of guests, partly to demonstrate a cavalier attitude toward material wealth, and partly as an ego boost to demonstrate their superiority. On the other hand, to accept such generosity from an outsider, especially a foreigner, would deflate their ego by putting them in an inferior position.

Many foreigners coming to Japan have an image of the Japanese as being rich and generous, and the more parsimonious of them will deliberately hold back in restaurants and other places until the Japanese pick up the bills. Usually, foreign visitors don't have to go to such extremes to avoid paying a bill. The Japanese generally regard themselves as the host unless they are specifically invited out. I have often seen and been involved in outright struggles with Japanese over food and bar bills, and there is a time to give in and a time to pay your own way.

There is the strong feeling among the Japanese that if they pay such bills they have demonstrated their sincerity, generosity, kindness, and goodwill. But the foreign businessman should set a limit on the amount and volume of hospitality he will accept. Otherwise he will lose respect in their eyes.

27

Inside a Japanese Company

The organization or structure of Japanese companies is simple enough, and is also similar enough to Western companies that it can be misleading to those who are unfamiliar with the inner workings of Japanese firms and who presume they also function very much like foreign firms.

Companies are normally divided into *bu* (buu) or departments, and *ka* (kah.) or sections. Each department is made up of a number of sections. There are the usual departments divided by function, and ranging from advertising to sales. Sections within departments are also divided by function, and are the key working units in all companies.

Each *bu* (department) is headed by a *bucho* (buu choe), or department head, who usually goes by the English title of general manager, and is the equivalent of a vice-president in American companies. His assistant, *bucho dairi* (buu choe die-ree), is the deputy general manager.

Each *ka* (section) is headed by a manager called *kacho* (kah choe), who may have one or two assistants called *kakaricho* (kah-kah-ree-choe), or supervisors. Each section is made up of a team of six or eight to sixteen or more people who all do basically the same kind of work. Team members consist of men and women ranging from the youngest recruits right out of school up to the *kacho* who is usually a veteran of at least fourteen years. It usually takes around eight years to reach the level of *kakaricho*.

Desks in the *ka* are usually arranged in an elongated box fashion, with the *kacho* at the head and the supervisors to his right or left. The lowest ranking member of the team is normally at the foot of the box. As team members pile up longevity, they gradually work their way up the line of desks.

The *ka* making up a department are arranged more or less classroom style, with the department chief at the head of the room—usually farthest from the door and often with his back to a window. The more important the section, the more centrally located it may be in relation to the desk of the department head.

The one Japanese department that few if any foreign companies have is the *Somu Bu* (soe-muu buu) or General Affairs Department. This is the catchall department. It handles company mail, maintains the company files and stock ledgers, coordinates interdepartmental relations, handles public relations and steers visitors to the right section. The first contact with most larger Japanese companies is with the *Somu Bu*.

Since it is the *ka* that produce the work in Japanese companies, the *kacho* in all of the sections and departments that have anything to do with a project are the key people with whom the outsider must interface. Just talking to the higher executives and *bucho* is generally not enough. It is always advisable and often essential that one meet and cultivate a close relationship with several *kacho* in a company with which you are doing business or want to do business.

Other typical departments in Japanese companies:

Accounting–*Keiri Bu* (kay-e-ree buu)
Advertising–*Koho Bu* (koe-hoe buu)
International–*Kokusai Bu* (koe-kuu-sie buu)
Personnel–*Jinji Bu* (jeen-jee buu)
Planning–*Kikaku Bu* (kee-kah-kuu buu)
Production–*Seizo Bu* (say-e-zoe buu)
Public Relations–*Shogai Bu* (show-guy buu)
Purchasing–*Shizai Bu* (she-zie buu)
Sales–*Eigyo Bu* (a-ee-g'yoe buu)

Larger Japanese companies have three levels of employees—the *yakuin* (yah-kuu-een), or the executives from director on up; the *bu/kacho* (buu-kah-choe) or middle and lower managers, made of the section and department heads and their assistants; and the *hira shain* (hee-rah-shah-een) or ''level'' employees who have no rank.

The table of organization in a large company looks like this:

Stockholders–*Kabunushi* (kah-buu-nuu-she)
Board of Directors–*Torishimari yakkai*
  (toe-ree-she-mah-ree yahck-kie)
Chairman of the Board–*Kaicho* (kie-choe)
Representative Director–*Daihyo Torishimari Yaku*
  (die-h'yoe toe-ree-shee-mah-ree yah-kuu)
President–*Shacho* (shah-choe)
Director & Executive Vice President–*Senmu Torishimari Yaku* (same-muu toe-ree-she-mah-ree yah-kuu)

Director & Senior Vice President–*Jomu Torishimari Yaku* (joe-muu toe-ree-she-mah-ree yah-kuu)

Standing Auditor–*Jonin Kansayaku* (joe-neen kahn-sah-yah-kuu)

Department Head–*Bucho* (buu choe)

Section Head–*Kacho* (kah-choe)

Supervisor–*Kakaricho* (kah-kah-ree-choe)

Unranked employees–*Hira Shain* (hee-rah shah-een)

Full-time employees–*Sei Shain* (say-e-shah-een)

Part-time employees–*Arubaito* (ah-ruu-buy-toe)

A representative director *(daihyo torishimari yaku)* has power of attorney to act in the name of the company, and larger firms may have more than one. In some companies, ranking *bucho* may also be directors. Generally, all of the directors of Japanese companies are in-house directors. In addition to regular department heads *(bucho)*, some companies have *senmon bucho* (same-moan buu choe), or "specialty chiefs" who are given the title because of their special skills, but have no department under them.

A primary difference in Japanese and most Western companies is that top executives in larger Japanese firms, regardless of their title, do not manage or direct their companies from the top down. They do little or no "managing" in the usual Western sense of the term, which connotes going around and giving orders to people.

Top executives set the general policies of their companies, but planning and day-to-day management is in the hands of middle and lower management who use a consensus approach to decision-making. In Japanese companies, almost no manager tells anybody what to do. New employees are given orientation, but they are expected to learn their actual work by watching and asking co-workers who are more advanced, and by doing.

Presidents of Japanese companies often say they spend most of their time training and nurturing future managers in the company, and frequently taking part in company interviews and orientations. One of the primary obligations of many *bucho* is to identify especially capable people in their departments and help groom them for higher management positions.

Foreign businessmen proposing to do business with the Japanese should keep in mind that impressing the chairman of the board, the president, or other high-level executives is a nice thing to do, but that in all likelihood it will be the *kacho* and *bucho* who determine whether or not their projects will fly—based on their research, evaluation, and recommendations.

Again, the ideal situation is to have an introduction to a top-level executive—from someone on or very near the same level—and then after the formalities and as much of a get-acquainted session as is practical, ask him to introduce you to the appropriate staff.

Another characteristic of larger Japanese companies that you should always keep in mind is the problem of direct communication between departments. It is almost always advisable, and sometimes critical, for you to develop close working relationships with the heads of several departments and sections to ensure that your project is understood and receives proper treatment.

28

The Spirit of Japanese Companies

Every Japanese company of any size has a particular image of itself, as well as a company policy, that influences its behavior and provides insights into how to approach and deal with it. In the simplest of terms, a company that sees itself as a dealer in seaweed is not likely to show any interest in handling shoes. But in Japan the concept is far more subtle and complex, particularly in large firms, and familiarity with a company's self-image can be a major asset in approaching it.

There are two key terms used in reference to the character and goals of larger Japanese firms: *shakun* (shah-koon) and *shaze* (shah-zay), which are similar in meaning and sometimes more or less interchangeable. *Shaze* refers to a company's ideals or the principles that guide it in establishing its policies and conducting itself in relation to the community at large as well as the marketplace. The *shaze* is generally expressed in the form of a motto. *Shakun,* which means something like "company precepts," refers to a company's philosophy, and may be written in the form of "commandments."

The *shaze/shakun* of manufacturers of consumer goods and service companies is particularly important because they are essential parts of their public image, which must be bright, strong, and positive to elicit the right response from the buying public.

A careful study of the *shaze/shakun* of any company, and being able to discuss them in a knowledgeable fashion, can be a big plus for the foreign businessman from several angles. One, it reveals a great deal about the personality of the company and the role it sees itself playing in the marketplace and world at large. Two, it provides useful insights in dealing with the company because it allows you to tailor your approach and relationship to be compatible with—and enhance—the company philosophy and goals.

Showing familiarity with the *shakun/shaze* of a company at the first meeting can be a very big boost for you in the eyes of your contacts. It demonstrates clearly that you are more than a one-dimensional person. The Japanese appreciate you having done your homework, and are more likely to pay attention to you since you have, in part at least, qualified yourself as someone who could be a sincere, trustworthy contact.

If you do not have a company motto or creed, no matter how small your company might be, you should give some thought to creating one. Actually, the *shakun* and *shaze* are as much for the benefit of employees as they are the public, since they help define a company's goals, thereby providing employees with guidelines for their own behavior.

By having a company creed you send a strong message to the Japanese that there is an intangible substance—a deeper dimension—to both you and your company, and this helps reduce the stereotypical image they are likely to have of you and your firm.

29

Making the First Contact

Your first contact with a Japanese company is crucial. The best scenario is for one or more Japanese firms to have become aware of you and interested in you from indirect, unrelated sources, such as a story about your company or project in the news media, or one of their own "scouts" or agents picking up on your story and reporting it— resulting in the Japanese side initiating the first contact.

You can make this happen, or at least encourage it, by deliberate action on your part—arranging for news coverage in media most likely to be monitored by the kind of Japanese contact you are looking for; tapping into the information-gathering network of the company you would like to have as a contact and planting the seed that would attract the company to you; exhibiting at trade shows; advertising in the appropriate trade media.

While there are numerous advantages to having the Japanese side make the first direct move, such as pinpointing for you the individuals within the company who are involved and shortening the period of time usually consumed by these initial steps, it is still essential that you qualify any firm that approaches you. Companies attracted by potential new projects may be too small, too big, not well positioned, or be in some totally unrelated area, and any prospect should be carefully checked out, including large, well-known companies. Large companies often look into things in which they have only marginal interest, keep would-be suppliers or partners dangling for months to years, and frequently tie up projects that are not given enough priority to get them off the ground floor.

When the first contact is from the Japanese side, the bigger and better known your company, the more likely it is that you will be contacted by at least a *bu cho* (department head). If you are a good-sized company, higher-level executives, at least on a director level, and higher if your company is really big, are generally brought into the picture if their interest is quite serious. Depending on the circumstances, the CEO could be brought in—especially in smaller companies. If they go this far, you can be assured that they have had several meetings about you, and have agreed to follow up.

If the company is a major firm and you are introduced to the president or CEO, you should not attempt to make your pitch to him—unless you are clearly invited to do so, which would be a considerable break from the norm since presidents and CEOs do not generally get involved in the business directly.

The next best bet is to have a third party, a consultant or agent or contact (such as a banker), make the first approach, introduce your company and your project, and get a hearing on whether or not the Japanese side wants to pursue the contact. If they do, obviously they will agree to meet you. This is the category of approach (from the outside) that the Japanese generally prefer because they are far more comfortable in dealing with go-betweens during the early stages of any relationship.

Third in the preferred order is for you to make the first direct contact. It is vitally important that this contact be through or with an introduction, which, if at all possible, includes the name, title, and department of the man you write or call. If your introduction does not specify the man you are to see, your call or letter will be taken by the *Somu Bu* or General Affairs Department, upon which you must depend to put you in touch with the right person.

A letter or fax not addressed to a specific individual or department, if the contents are clear, may find its way into the right hands, and then again it may not, depending on who gets hold of it, what they understand of it, and who they think should take care of it. In some cases, their reaction may be based more on internal politics or rivalries than on your own best interests. Larger Japanese companies receive thousands of letters every month, many of them in obscure languages. Most are never answered simply because it would be costly and nonproductive to do so.

If you telephone and are unable to specify whom you want to talk to, you end up having to explain yourself to a receptionist, a clerk, or other low-level member of the General Affairs Department. Depending on their perception of what you want, you can easily be passed around to two, three, or more individuals, in some cases all in the General Affairs Department, which screens cold contacts from the outside.

It is common for this department to agree to meet outsiders, listen to their presentations, sometimes spread out over two or three occasions, and then announce that there is no interest in your project or that they will introduce you to the proper department. You may not be told directly that there is no interest, since that would be considered impolite. A common reaction is for the Japanese side to say they will consider the idea, and then leave you dangling—the assumption being, of course, that your "belly" will tell you what they did not.

Obviously, it is important for you to avoid this kind of situation by determining in advance—or having someone determine for you—whom you should see in a Japanese company.

30

Getting the Bow Down

Bowing as a form of greeting, expressing farewell and appreciation is the one aspect of Japanese etiquette that everyone notices, not only because it is visible but also because it often creates awkward situations between Japanese and foreigners—and regularly causes a variety of mishaps. It is common for people walking in front of you, frequently in very crowded situations, to stop abruptly in their tracks and bow to someone suddenly confronting them, making it impossible for you to avoid colliding with their rear ends.

When foreigners who are not conditioned to just bowing are being introduced to several Japanese at the same time, they will often automatically try to combine shaking hands with everyone in the party and bowing. When the Japanese side is not Westernized enough to quickly and efficiently respond to proffered hands, one may find oneself in a mess of hands and bowing bodies. This can be even further complicated when the foreigners try to exchange name cards with each of the Japanese at the same time—which they usually do.

Part of the problem is that the foreign side moves too quickly and often in no particular order, not giving the Japanese enough time to react. In the Japanese way, bowing and exchanging name cards are done more slowly, more formally, avoiding confusion. Among themselves the Japanese usually know, or are able to quickly discern, the order of rank of the people they are meeting, and bow to them in the proper order. Each move thereafter is made in as controlled a manner as the space and situation allows, as they alternately face and bow to each individual.

In larger groups, the groups bow to each other at the same time, which is a lot more efficient than shaking hands. Later, during a break, for example, individuals will introduce themselves one by one.

If you are being introduced to a small group, say three to five or six, the challenge is to identify the order of rank of the people you are being introduced to (the ranking person is very often the oldest one in the group), and then to slowly and deliberately position yourself more or less in front of each one of them, hand them your name card, and then combine a modest bow with shaking hands. In case of a larger group, say eight or ten, that you are going to be dealing with individually—as opposed to an audience—just continue the above protocol until you have met them all, without rushing things.

Again, you can avoid making the meeting awkward by doing it slowly and deliberately—which is the proper way in the first place.

Using the bow as a farewell is usually easier to master, since it does not involve name cards or giving your name and is much more casual. Generally one shakes hands with the individuals departing, and then when they turn for a last look a modest bow is good etiquette. About the only foreigners who regularly use the bow to express appreciation (thanks) are those who have become Japanized in their behavior, by osmosis, and do it automatically, without thinking about it. It doesn't hurt, and it might help.

31

The Name-Card Game

As mentioned, foreigners who are not well-practiced in Japanese-style greeting formalities often add to the confusion when meeting several people by attempting to bow, shake hands, and pass out name cards at the same time. Again the key is to do things one at a time, slowly, deliberately, with some style.

I'm sure by this time everyone with even the remotest interest in Japan is aware of the use and importance of name cards in Japan. They are, in fact, much more important in Japan than in most countries because they establish rank as well as identity, and knowledge of rank is vital to the way the Japanese relate to and react to others. But there are some pointers beyond just how to exchange name cards that play a role in overall Japanese etiquette in business.

First, it is advisable to have your cards printed in your native language on one side and in phonetic Japanese on the other side. English especially is difficult for Japanese to pronounce because the spelling often doesn't provide a clue. Having the name of your company, particularly if it is not a well-known name, as well as your title rendered in Japanese is also important to complete the identification.

If your cards are especially well-designed and well-printed, so much the better because this makes a solid, favorable impression. Colored paper stock or other materials are also acceptable and often beneficial—if they are not too far-out. I have been using my photograph on my own cards since the 1950s. They always elicit favorable comments, and beginning in the 1980s a few of the more individualist Japanese began picking up on the idea. Most Japanese in the creative professions have very individualized cards.

It is customary in Japan to use card cases, and this is a practice worth following. Among other things, it keeps your cards from getting dog-eared. A two-compartment case is best—one for yours and one for theirs.

Obviously when you are meeting Japanese it is both polite and makes common sense to hand your card to them with the Japanese-language side up and facing them, so they can read it without turning it over or around. Also, strict etiquette calls for the use of both hands in both giving and receiving cards, at least when you begin the ceremony. It is now common to extend the card with just one hand, and to accept it with one hand but then hold it in both hands when reading it.

It is not customary for name cards to be put away immediately, especially if you are sitting down or sit down soon after meeting. The practice is to place them on the coffee table or meeting table in front of you so you can look at the names and titles of the people you've just met to help you remember them.

Probably the most common breach of name-card etiquette committed by foreigners is to literally "deal" their cards out as if they were playing poker, tossing or sliding them across tables. It may seem like nitpicking or carrying formality too far to bring this up, but dispensing name cards in this manner graphically demonstrates an ignorance of local etiquette at least, and a cavalier or even arrogant attitude toward it at worst. As awkward and as wasteful as it might seem to get up from your chair and take the necessary steps to be able to hand your card to each individual, it is the wise and rational thing to do and will be to your benefit.

32

Getting Acquainted: the First Steps

The duration and content of your first meeting will vary, depending on who set it up, and whether or not the Japanese side already knows something about you and your project. Typically the first meeting is a get-acquainted session, but some companies now speed up this process—to save their time rather than the visitor's. The first few minutes should be kept on a relaxed social level and then you should express your appreciation for them taking time to see you, say you know how busy they are, and then diplomatically ask how much of their time you may have.

If the Japanese side has not been briefed and you are starting from scratch, it is essential that you first identify yourself thoroughly, including a complete explanation of your relationship with the person or persons who introduced you to their company, why you have targeted their company in the first place, and lastly, the broad outlines of your project or proposition.

If they have already been informed in detail, and particularly if they approached you, you can presume you are talking to the right people and can generally get down to business after a few minutes of pleasantries and getting acquainted.

Presuming that you have your first meeting set up with the right department (in a larger Japanese company), it will generally be with the manager or general manager of the department (these titles are used more or less interchangeably, depending on company policy), and with one or more assistants.

Once you have described your project in general terms, without asking for or expecting any kind of response from the Japanese side, you should end the first meeting on a light note, commenting that you look forward to meeting with them again after they have had time to consider your proposal. It is also essential that you have your proposal in writing, preferably in a bound book or notebook form, and leave one or more copies for the Japanese side to study in detail.

There is virtually no chance that the Japanese side will make any kind of decision or commitment on the first hearing of a presentation, other than to look at it carefully and get back to you. With very rare exceptions, such as in entrepreneurial companies still operated by a founder who is a strong one-man manager, individual Japanese, no matter how high their positions, do not make decisions on their own. Every subject is discussed at length with all of the managers who would be involved with any aspect of the undertaking, a process that can take weeks to months.

The normal routine, when a Japanese company is interested in a project brought in from the outside, is for them to meet anywhere from three or four to ten or fifteen times with the presenters, gradually adding more people to their team or bringing in substitutes until all of their key managers have been involved in the presentation and discussions. This generally means that the foreign side must basically make the same presentation several times.

After the Japanese side has heard and/or read all of the proposal, they invariably have questions, sometimes dozens to hundreds of them, depending on the complexity of the project. Different individuals on the Japanese team, who may not attend all of the sessions, often ask the same questions, sometimes phrased a little differently and sometimes not, requiring the foreign side to repeat itself a number of times.

The key to getting through this stage is patience, plus providing the additional information requested as expeditiously as possible, and holding as many in-

dividual talks as you can with th
department chiefs (more about this
additional information requested by
is something they need for the cust
trademark offices, or the ministries
your particular product or service.

This sometimes gets into proprietary ....s that are
sensitive, and you may want to determine, from outside sources, that the extra information they want is in
fact necessary in order for them to abide by government regulations.

33

How to Recognize "No"

One of the most frustrating
experiences the foreign businessman can have in
Japan is to get involved in any kind of presentation or
negotiations, and not know when he is wasting his
time.

This situation arises because the Japanese often cannot bring themselves to turn anyone away outright,
with a simple "no, thank you" or "sorry, that's not
for us." It is then compounded because the unconditioned foreigner does not recognize the subtle verbal
and non-verbal clues dropped by the Japanese—who

sending "no, no, no" loud and clear within
utes of the beginning of a presentation.

Knowing why the Japanese will almost never say
"no, thank you" is of no particular help. The key, of
course, is picking up on the negative signals. The most
obvious one—and the one that is the closest to a
specific turndown—is to have someone say, usually
with a strained expression, that something would be
muzukashii (muu-zuu-kah-she-e), or "difficult." When
you hear this you can bet your last yen that you are not
going to get across the moat, much less penetrate the
castle.

Sometimes the reaction is expressed non-verbally,
in which case you must be a good face-reader and sensitive to voice tones. When traditional Japanese
"politeness" prevents them from going any further
than this, they will often end the meeting by saying
they will consider your proposition—using the term
kangaete okimasu (kahn-guy-tay oh-kee-mahss), which
literally means "I will think about it." It does not
mean they will do anything more than just think about
it—in other words, it is a polite "no."

In the meantime, the Japanese are very much
aware that the foreign visitor has not understood their
message, because he (the foreigner) continues pitch-
ing, invariably with a degree of enthusiasm and
"logical thinking" that repels the Japanese. Thus the
longer the foreigner persists, the stronger the mental
block the Japanese build around their fort.

Another sign that a perceptive visitor might pick up on early in the session is that the Japanese side asks no questions and allows him to babble on. When the unperceptive foreigner finally runs down (and some will repeat themselves at the end in a closing pitch) another obvious sign that he has gotten nowhere is when the Japanese do not suggest or readily agree to a follow-up meeting.

Not surprisingly, there are numerous ways of saying "no" in several words: I'll do my best, I'll talk to the senior director about it, etc. In fact, the word for "no," *iie* (ee-eh), is almost never used. The practice is to use the negative form of verbs and other words. Are you going? *Ikimasu ka* (E-kee-mahss kah?). I'm not going. *Ikimasen* (E-kee-mah-sin). Similarly, the plain word "yes," *hai* (hi), is seldom used by itself.

Learning how to "read" meetings with Japanese is not easy, especially when the foreigner is speaking through an interpreter, because there is always the additional tendency for the interpreter to soften the impact of any negative comments by the Japanese side. It may be equally difficult when the Japanese side speaks adequate or very good English because he often chooses to be even more polite, not use the key words at all, and beam pleasantly throughout the presentation.

It is also very common for foreigners who speak quite good Japanese to become victims of this trap because they are not aware of the specific Japanese psychology and etiquette involved, or because they are unable to escape their own cultural conditioning and accept what they are hearing or seeing.

After you have made your presentation, there is a way to avoid keeping yourself on edge about the Japanese response if there is any doubt at all in your mind. A week or so later have a third party call the person you talked to, express your appreciation for his courtesy and time, and inquire, in the subtle way that is appropriate, about his reaction to you and your business.

This query should be made in Japanese and generally having a Japanese make it is best, but a foreigner whose language ability is good and who knows what special expressions to use in these cases can usually get a clear response.

34

Role of the Greeting Ritual

One of the most important parts of the personal side of business in Japan is the *aisatsu* (aye-sot-sue), or ritualized greeting that is required to develop and maintain good relations with clients and business associates.

In its simplest form the *aisatsu* is just a greeting; the

kind in which you would drop by the office of a business associate just to say hello because you happen to be in the neighborhood. The next step up is a visit to offer your congratulations to someone on some auspicious event—a promotion, recovery from an illness, return from an overseas assignment, some laudable business accomplishment, etc., in which case the motive—that of nurturing the relationship in order to obtain some direct benefit—becomes much clearer.

Another version of *aisatsu:* After outsiders have approached a Japanese company on a section or departmental level and it appears that some kind of a deal is going to be worked out—or the Japanese company has taken the initiative and wants the relationship—it is part of Japanese protocol to bring in directors and, in major programs, the president or chairman, for an *aisatsu* with representatives of the outside firm.

The most conspicuous and perhaps important use of the *aisatsu* in keeping business ties tight is at the beginning of each new year when it is a sanctified custom to pay your respects to clients and other valued business contacts, thanking them for their patronage and goodwill the previous year and asking them specifically to continue the relationship during the new year. This custom is known as *aisatsu mawari* (aye-sotsue mah-wah-ree), which literally means ''greeting go-around.'' In other words, one goes around from company to company, going through the stylized ritual of bowing to clients and affiliated businessmen, in every case using the same traditional expression: *Sakunen ju wa taihen o-sewa ni narimashita. Mata konnen mo yoroshiku o-negai itashimasu* (Sah-kuu nane juu wah tie-hane oh-say-wah nee nah-ree-mahssh-tah. Mah-tah kone-nane moe yoe-roe-ssh-kuu oh-nay-gay ee-tah-she-mahss). This translates loosely as, ''We are deeply obligated to you for your patronage/support/help last year. We humbly ask that you favor us again this year.''

This is a custom that foreign businessmen can quickly adopt in their relations with the Japanese. It requires no special expertise (the greeting can be in English for that matter), and it is very meaningful to the Japanese because it demonstrates your sincerity, and reassures them that you are a man who can be trusted to do what is right at the right time. Of course, it is even more impressive if you learn the above set phrase in Japanese, and use it at the appropriate time.

35

Seeing Behind the Facade

In Japanese culture the practice of ''putting on a face'' for the public, of concealing your real thoughts behind a carefully constructed facade of dress and protocol, has been one of the key facets of life. The foundation for this type of behavior was laid during the long feudal period when interpersonal relations were strictly governed by meticulously graded class and rank and an even more meticulously detailed etiquette that applied to virtually every act of life.

Presenting the right "face" at the right time was vital to survival in a very literal sense, so people became masters at masking their feelings and their true desires behind a public facade or *tatemae* (tah-tay my), which originally meant the ceremonial erection of the framework of a house.

In a business sense, *tatemae* refers to the image that one presents to outsiders, whether in a negotiating session or just in general. One of the keys to succeeding in business in Japan is to develop considerable skill in seeing behind the *tatemae* to perceive what the real situation is, or what the individual concerned really wants.

A *tatemae* front is also constantly used by the Japanese to conceal negative factors or to cover up actions or events they do not want to do or reveal openly. This requires even more experience and cultural sensitivity to discern.

Just about everybody postures and puts on an act that is *tatemae,* but generally far less so than the Japanese. The typical Western businessman, for example, is generally motivated by a high sense of fairness and prides himself on being candid; putting all of his cards on the table, as the saying goes. Not so the Japanese. They are conditioned to reveal as little as they can about their intentions, often concealing them behind a sophisticated facade, until they find out as much as possible about what the other side wants, and also until they determine where the consensus lies in their own group (since they do not want to be seen as being out of step). *Tatemae* could also be described as the world seen through rose-colored glasses, carefully crafted for the outsider's benefit. Extrapolating a little further, the Japan that most foreigners see is a master-piece of *tatemae* that hides a very different reality.

There is generally no fast, direct way one can get behind a *tatemae* and discern the true feelings or inten-tions of a Japanese negotiating team or an individual Japanese during the first and early stages of an en-counter. But the facade is not necessarily meant to deceive. It is also used simply to "cover" things until "reality" emerges from the consensus process.

Once you do get past *tatemae,* or your Japanese con-tacts reach the stage where they themselves discard the facade and reveal the "true situation" to you, you have reached *honne* (hoan nay) or the "honest voice." Achieving *honne* in your relations with Japanese businessmen is very much like pursuing enlighten-ment. It is often not so much a verbal process as an in-tuitive or visceral process that just grows on you. It often happens that virtually all you see and hear in your daytime dealings with Japanese is *tatemae. Honne* often comes into play only at night when you are living it up in a cabaret.

36

The All-Important Pre-Agreement Meetings

Japanese concern with interpersonal harmony and especially avoiding public displays of disagreement led to the development of *uchiawase* (uu-chee-ah-wah-say), or figuratively "coming to agreement in advance," into a vital part of all social and work activity. In the social sense, this is nothing more than advance planning, which everyone does, but when applied to business, particularly to business with foreign companies, it becomes part of the negotiating process that foreign businessmen need to know about.

All business projects in Japan, of whatever nature, are preceded by one or more (and usually it is more) *uchiawase,* which is the main reason why it is so important to provide a Japanese company with all the pertinent information prior to meeting them to negotiate any kind of arrangement. The more information they have been given, and the stronger it presents your case, the more likely you are to achieve your goals.

The Japanese way is to settle all of the issues of any project during the *uchiawase* stage—which, again, is why they ask for so much information in advance—and then come together officially for formal recognition of the agreement. Foreign businessmen who are aware of what is going on in the background can help their own case by making themselves available for—and requesting—unofficial meetings, including evenings out in the *mizu shobai* during this period.

After an agreement is reached, Japanese businessmen traditionally celebrate with an *uchiage* (uu-chee-ah-gay), which literally means ''shoot off,'' as in fireworks, but in this case means more like ''send off,'' in terms of the project to be launched. In the old days this ceremony included the ritual clapping of hands in a rhythmic cadence, along with a lot of drinking. Now the hand-clapping may be skipped, but not the drinking.

37

Revolving the Roots

The *uchiawase* process is part of Japan's group- or team-oriented approach to decision-making by consensus, which is known in its entirety as *nemawashi* (nay-mah-wah-she), which literally means "root revolving," or the spinning or turning of a root.

The inference in this term is that the proposed project or subject of discussion (the root) is "revolved" (or spun or turned) around and around by all of the people concerned until they have become thoroughly familiar with it, have asked all the questions they might have, and made all of the suggestions they might want to make.

This is the aspect of decision-making in Japan that often confuses and frustrates foreigners, because it takes so long and because so many people are involved, it is often impossible to find out from an individual contact how the project is faring at any one time or stage.

The most important people in the early stages of the *nemawashi* process are the *kacho* (section chiefs), who are the ones generally responsible for doing all of the research and the recommendations to higher-level management. Sometimes, particularly in the case of a major project in which the involvement of the company would be on a large scale, the man in charge of the project may be a deputy department chief or even department head.

Generally, it is only during the *uchiawase/nemawashi* process that the outsider can bring influence to bear on the decision-making process. That is the reason why it is vital the Japanese side have all the pertinent information about a project, and that they understand it completely—and is also the reason why it is important to stay in close—usually unofficial—contact with key individuals during this process (meetings over lunch, dinner, or drinks, etc.), to add more new insights and ammunition, without being pushy. But be aware that if you come on too strong, you can do more damage than good.

38

The Written Document System

Once the section chiefs and department managers have done their thing, their proposals or recommendations are put into written form and passed on to their counterparts in other sections or departments, who in turn add their comments, if any, and pass them on. Generally, all of the section chiefs, all of the deputy department chiefs, and all of the department chiefs who would be involved in implementing any aspect of the proposal get their turn at the proposal.

In earlier years, the written form of a proposal was generally referred to as a *ringi-sho* (reen-ghee show) or "written document," and the process was known as the *ringi seido* (reen-ghee say-e-doe) or "written document system," or "request for decision system." It

114

was a very formal affair, in which each participant had to sign off on each document with his official name stamp or *hanko* (hahn-koe). Those who disapproved of the proposal would refuse to stamp it; if they were not totally opposed but had strong reservations, they would put their stamp on upside down.

Over the years the process has become less bureaucratic in some companies, some no longer refer to the process they use as the *ringi* system, and some hold meetings instead of circulating documents, but the process of approval or disapproval of a proposal remains essentially the same—it must be presented to all concerned, in all of its ramifications, and unanimous agreement is sought before it is accepted.

Once again the most critical period of any project being considered by a Japanese company—no matter where it comes from—is when the *kacho* are doing their research, planning, and drafting of whatever proposal they are going to make. If the proposal has come from the outside, this is the point at which it is vital to make sure that the person in charge has every possible detail and insight that you can provide him.

It is also extremely important to find out from the initiating section chief or deputy department chief who the other key people are in the process—who he will be circulating the proposal to or holding meetings with on his level—so that you can also meet them and—without being obnoxious or crude—do your best to make sure they also have all of the pertinent facts as you see them, before they reach the final stage of decision-making.

If your relationship with the key "window man" is good (if he obviously appreciates the potential of the project and is pursuing it diligently), he will be very cooperative as far as getting input from you is concerned, and will generally cooperate in introducing you to the other players, since having committed himself to some degree, he will also have a vested interest in getting the approval of his colleagues.

In going beyond the window man, however, you must exercise extreme caution not to undercut him or in any way give the impression that you are going around or over him. Any such action or impression will invariably result in his losing face and will sour your relationship with him.

While on the subject of written proposals, it should be noted that Japanese businessmen write very few memos—because of the complexity of the Japanese language and the difficulty of writing it, the absence in most companies of secretaries in the Western sense, and the fact that most Japanese executives prefer to manage with the spoken word and direct face-to-face contact instead of cold type.

All this combined is, of course, why the Japanese have so many meetings in the course of a business day, and also part of the reason why they prefer large "open" offices, without separate compartments or dividers, in which everybody in the place can be seen and where communication can circulate freely throughout the room more or less at the same time, with everyone knowing what the others are doing, how they are behaving, who they are meeting.

39

The Importance of Following Up

Once you have made an approach to a Japanese company it is essential that you do a lot of follow-up in a systematic and deliberate way. This, of course, demonstrates the level of your interest, but more importantly it is necessary for you to continue providing positive input. As mentioned earlier, going through your main contact man to his counterparts in other sections and departments is often the key to getting the consensus you want.

Many foreign businessmen who go to Japan to make presentations fail to do sufficient follow-up after their return home either because they think there is nothing more for them to say or because they believe the next step is up to the Japanese side. The point is, failure to keep regular contact with a potential Japanese customer or partner results in a kind of vacuum in which you are soon forgotten and action is likely to wind down and maybe stop altogether.

117

The Japanese do not feel comfortable or confident in a relationship unless there is frequent, personal contact, and especially so in the first stages of a budding new relationship. To prevent the creation of a gap, it is important that you have some kind of contact at least every other week until the bonds are well cemented. This contact can be a phone call, fax, or letter. Nowadays, a fax often takes precedence over a phone call because you can say exactly what you want and there is a record of your comments.

These follow-ups can include such things as additional information that relate to your joint interests, or expressions of your readiness to provide such information should they need or want it. In dealing with the Japanese it is important to keep in mind that business is done on a very personal level.

40

How to Use Interpreters

Using *tsuyaku* (t'sue-yah-kuu) interpreters effectively requires a considerable amount of skill that usually comes only with experience. But being forewarned will significantly shorten this learning curve.

First, it is important that the foreign businessman

understand and accept the fact that good interpreting on such important issues as business and politics is very difficult and demanding, and that really first-rate interpreters are exceedingly rare.

A second important point to keep in mind is that as long as it is the Japanese side that provides the interpreter you are at a disadvantage that ranges from moderate to very serious. When the interpreter belongs to the other side, over and above the fact that he or she is usually not really good at it and often fails to fully transmit what each side says, you must keep in mind that the non-professionally trained interpreter will to varying degrees ''re-interpret'' what both sides say, especially what the foreign side says, to suit his or her own position, habits, beliefs, aims, and often social rank in relation to the Japanese side.

A Japanese interpreter provided by the Japanese side will also be under significant etiquette constraints to ''sanitize'' the conversation to avoid upsetting anyone, thereby often failing to translate both meanings and feelings—leaving both sides dissatisfied since they readily recognize from the tone of voice and by face-reading that there is some passion involved.

The first rule in using interpreters is therefore to provide your own whenever humanly possible. The second rule is that regardless of whose intepreter you are using, it is very important that you talk with them at length before the beginning of any meeting, not only to judge the level of their ability, but especially to brief them in as much detail as possible about the subject matter you are going to cover.

Ideally, you would be able to provide interpreters with a written version of your presentations in advance. You should then question them closely to make sure they understand it in your language. If you must, in fact, depend upon interpreters provided by the Japanese side, you should not hesitate to request that you be permitted to meet them before the beginning of any meeting to discuss your material. If an individual assigned by a Japanese company to act as interpreter does not want to meet you, is reluctant to do so, or is prevented from doing so, you are already in trouble.

There is a tendency for people to over-use interpreters and tire them out, no doubt presuming that it is easy work—just talking. But doing a thoroughly professional job of interpreting is one of the most demanding intellectual and emotional exercises one can engage in. Sessions should not go beyond two hours without breaks. For day-long programs you should have a minimum of two interpreters so they can spell each other.

Another thing to avoid is attempts at canned humor, especially ethnic jokes which often do not translate well even when the interpreter is a master. Spontaneous humor, especially the self-deprecating kind, is just as much appreciated in Japan as anywhere else, and an appropriate remark that fits the occasion can get you just as much mileage.

41

More About Failing to Follow Through

One of the biggest weaknesses of foreign businessmen attempting to initiate a relationship with Japanese companies is failure to follow through after the first and/or the second or successive meetings. This lapse derives from a combination of factors that, of course, come under the general heading of lack of knowledge about the way the Japanese do business.

But breaking the lapse down, we find that it begins with foreign businesses assuming that all they have to do is inform the Japanese side of a good business deal or area of potential and then sit back and wait for the Japanese to pick up the ball and run with it. That can happen, but generally it does not. Not having an established business relationship with the foreign company is often enough by itself to stop the Japanese side from taking any action, even when they find the proposition interesting.

The Japanese side *expects* the foreign company to follow up, to take all the steps necessary to establish an acceptable relationship, and to provide the Japanese company with all of the assurances and evidence they need to accept the foreign firm as a stable, trustworthy company they could deal with in confidence.

Another aspect of the problem is that foreign businessmen inexperienced in Japan are not aware of the personal factor in Japanese business relations; of how much personal time must be invested in establishing a business relationship. It does not begin and end with a good product and good price. These come after the personal ties are formed.

It is vital for the foreign side to keep in mind that initiating and nurturing a successful new business relationship with a Japanese company is something like planting and growing a fragile flower that requires regular, and sometimes daily, care. It is also like a marriage that breaks down quickly if the couple does not communicate and stroke each other regularly.

Another problem that often accompanies the failure-to-follow-through syndrome is lack of sufficient research and preparation prior to the first contact. As I noted in my book *How to Do Business with the Japanese,* the Japanese will research a project for six months or more before making the decision to do it, but once the decision is made they are prepared to implement it immediately. In contrast to this, foreign businessmen, and especially Americans it seems, will announce new projects and then spend six months or more researching and preparing before they are ready to start them.

When foreign companies hooked on this method approach a Japanese firm, which then turns out to be interested, they often find themselves needing six months or more of study and preparation before they can meet the expectations of the Japanese. This naturally suggests to the Japanese side that the foreign company is shortsighted, if not incompetent, and could well put a damper on their interest.

The message is: do your homework; make the contact; follow up as diligently and as frequently as you would in courting a very desirable mate.

42

Dealing at the Negotiating Table

The Japanese side expects— and usually insists—that the foreign side in a bargaining session present their case first. On the surface this may be offered as a gesture of courtesy—giving the other side the first shot. But in reality it is a well-practiced ploy to achieve an advantage, since it allows the Japanese side to adjust their responses in their favor. Of course, if the foreign side has initiated the contact and is the petitioner, it is natural that they go first. If you have been approached by a Japanese company, the shoe is obviously on the other foot.

When you are the initiator, the best negotiating approach is to first cover the proposed project in general, broad terms, letting the framework of what you propose sink in. Once this is done you may or may not get any feedback from the Japanese side. They may say they cannot comment until they get more specific details. Fair enough.

But on your second run-through when you do go into more specifics, you should open each main point up for discussion, pulling the Japanese side in and questioning them to draw out their thinking on that point.

It is important that you make any presentation slowly and clearly, using graphics and other supporting materials as much as possible, and that someone in your group keeps track of all the questions the Japanese side asks, as well as your answers. Invariably on the Japanese side there will be one or more people who do not participate in the dialogue, and do nothing but scribble notes, making it possible for them to thoroughly review the proceedings afterward.

Surprisingly, many foreign businessmen negotiating in Japan ask few if any questions of their Japanese opposites—sometimes, it seems, out of a misplaced sense of politeness. You should go into every session with a written list of questions to ask, and add to the list as the negotiations proceed. One of the reasons why so many foreign companies have problems with their Japanese partners after they go into business together is that the foreign side did not ask enough questions during the courting stage. This is often serious and can be fatal.

43

Killing with Silence

In Japanese negotiating protocol, long periods of silence are a part of the process. They are both a brief, unannounced, unofficial rest period as well as a strategic ploy during which both sides continue to feel each other out non-verbally. Members of the Japanese team will simply stop talking. Some will lean back and close their eyes, as if sleeping. They often get up and leave the table, returning to their desks or going to the toilet or whatever, without any sign. They will also hold whispered or low-voiced consultations in Japanese with other members of the team—especially when there is no one on the foreign side who understands Japanese.

The tactical aspect of this practice is known as *mokusatsu* (moh-kuu-sot-sue), which is usually translated as "killing with silence." The Japanese negotiators will go silent as a technique for drawing the other side out, to get them to give in to a point or make other concessions.

Americans in particularly seem to be especially susceptible to this tactic. Being aggressive and conditioned to expect things to move forward rapidly in clockwork fashion, they become increasingly uncomfortable even with a silence of only a few seconds, and begin talking, usually repeating themselves and often making concessions outright, or hinting that their position is not cut in stone. A silence of thirty seconds or so is enough to make many American negotiators panic.

The proper response to the *mokusatsu* ploy is to review your notes, refresh yourself if you need to, chat privately with a member of your own team, and let the scenario develop for two or three minutes. When the Japanese see that you are familiar with the strategy and are not going to give the store away, they will usually resume the discussions. Or, after sufficient time has elapsed for you to make your point (that you also know the art of *mokusatsu*), you can take the initiative and resume the meeting without losing any ground.

Another aspect of the use of time: Foreign negotiators should not state that they have a deadline and will be leaving on such-and-such a date. This gives the Japanese side the opportunity to bring increasing pressure on the foreign side simply by delaying things. The closer the deadline comes, the more apt the foreign side is to give in and accept the Japanese position. I have been involved in situations (not from the beginning!) in which the last points were agreed upon in a car on the way to the airport.

You can certainly let the Japanese know that time is important, and that if you cannot work out an acceptable relationship with them that you will go on to other prospects. But don't lock yourself in to where you have to accept what is offered because you "ran out of time."

44

Beware of Using Logic

In some forty years of living and working with Japanese, I have been faulted hundreds of times for trying to conduct myself in a logical manner—for almost always assuming that the well-ordered life, just as the successful business, is based on the principle that fact follows fact; that two plus two always equals four. In Japan it does not.

In fact, the Japanese are made very uncomfortable by logical thinking. In the Japanese context, feeling is more important than logical reasoning. They believe that an enterprise based on logical thinking cannot give proper due to the human element—recognizing, it seems, that human beings are generally illogical creatures.

To the Japanese, people are incapable of "heart-to-heart" communication and cannot use the "art of the belly" when they have their logic cap on. The Japanese equate logical thinking with independent thinking and independent thinking with inability to cooperate with others in a Japanese-style team effort.

The foreign businessman who stands up and uses good, solid logic to preach a sermon about the merits of his product or project is on safe enough ground. But he is soon in quicksand if he uses the same approach in proposing how the enterprise should be launched and managed. About the only effective solution is to downplay the "cold, hard reasoning" in all discussions, but quietly mix as much logic as possible in with the Japanese approach when implementing a project.

45

Mastering the Art of Business at Night

One of the most interesting aspects of business in Japan—and another key to doing it successfully—is what has traditionally been known as the *mizu shobai* (me-zuu show-bye) or "water business," which refers primarily to the nighttime entertainment trades—cabarets, bars, nightclubs, geisha inns, and hot baths, etc.

Both business and politics in Japan have long been associated with the *mizu shobai,* with deals planned and consummated in a *mizu shobai* setting instead of in an office or boardroom. One possible reason for this is that in the old days, private offices were virtually non-existent, and if one wanted to talk privately it was often better that it be done in a public place. Another possible reason is that the drinking of saké, the traditional Japanese alcoholic beverage, has also long been directly associated with formal events and ceremonies (just as alcoholic drinks have in Western societies), as a semi-sacred ritual that formalized decisions or actions.

A third factor is that the traditionally strict etiquette that prevailed in Japan made it either difficult or impossible for the Japanese to talk freely and frankly except when they were in recognized, sanctioned drinking places, could forget about *tatemae,* and really let their hair down. Japanese history is filled with anecdotes about famed political and business leaders meeting in red-light districts and geisha inns to carry on their business. These purveyors of sensual pleasure apparently symbolized the intimate nature of the relationship the businessmen desired to develop.

The role of the *mizu shobai* in politics and business in present-day Japan has not diminished, but the venue for businessmen is usually a cabaret instead of a brothel (politicians remain devoted patrons of the geisha). The change that overcomes the typical Japanese businessman in a cabaret, with its cadre of attractive hostesses and intimate ambience, is startling to see. From the formal, protocol-conscious organization man who behaves in a meticulously prescribed manner, the businessman becomes a playful playboy. He drinks, laughs, sings, dances, and behaves in a thoroughly licentious manner toward the cabaret girls who are there for his pleasure.

It is in the *mizu shobai* that Japanese cement and maintain the personal ties and emotional bonds that are so important to their business relationships. They do not—virtually cannot—feel at ease with other people or feel that they know them and can trust them until they have shared a number of cabaret, bathhouse or geisha inn experiences, because it is only on these occasions that they allow their own personal feelings and character to come out, and they presume it is the same with non-Japanese as well.

The ritual of drinking and letting go in the "water trade" is so important to the Japanese that even those who are not heavy drinkers and dedicated carousers will simulate the behavior in order to fit in, be accepted, and play the necessary game.

Foreign businessmen who become involved with the Japanese are invariably invited by their hosts or Japanese contacts to a cabaret or inn that calls in geisha. The first invitation is usually on the second or third day, after the visitors have had a good night's sleep and a day or so of meetings—during which decisions and/or judgments are only rarely made.

What is most likely to happen is that about two or three hours into the evening—and sometimes just as the party is breaking up—the key Japanese man will suddenly sober up, and very directly and pointedly comment on the negotiations at that point, either that they are going well or that there is a problem or obstacle that has to be overcome.

The Japanese side does not expect the foreign side to immediately start discussions. They are letting the foreign side know what is going on so the foreigner can think about it overnight and react to it the following day. As soon as these brief comments are made the Japanese will instantly revert to the role of playboy out on the town, without missing a beat.

46

The Importance of a Hidden Art

There is one key to doing business in Japan that can be a lot of fun if the foreigner will just put his heart (and a few other things) into it. This facet of the Japanese business world is known as *kakushi-gei* (kah-kuu-she-gay-e) or "hidden art," and refers to some personal skill—usually singing—which the individual businessman can demonstrate in public.

As already mentioned in the section on the *mizu shobai,* Japanese businessmen spend a lot of time in bars and cabarets. One of the most popular categories of nightspots are the *karaoke* (kah-rah-oh-kay) bars, where patrons are encouraged to take center stage and sing into a microphone in synch with piped in orchestra music.

In earlier times, learning how to sing was a part of the growing-up and educational process in Japan. Mothers taught children how to sing, and singing was practiced in school. People sang at parties, at festivals and at special ceremonies, in groups and individually. Most Japanese still do a lot of singing during their formative years, and almost any businessman has at least the courage, if not the skill, to stand up and sing a solo when the occasion arises.

But not content with just being a so-so singer, many Japanese practice discreetly, developing their *kakushi-gei* so that when they are called on to sing or when they volunteer to sing they will not be embarrassed and their friends will be pleasantly surprised.

There is probably not one lower- or middle-ranking manager in Japan who has not patronized a *karaoke* bar and taken his turn on the floor, crooning his most practiced tune. And visiting foreign businessmen are expected to take their turns as well!

Of course, the Japanese assume that all foreigners can sing at least as well as they can and have no special fears about getting up and performing in public. So saying "no" to an insistent host (whom you want to do business with) is very difficult.

To the Japanese businessman, carrying on and singing in a *karaoke* bar is therapy—therapy that he sorely needs to mitigate the strict behavior required of him at the office. It is, in fact, a marvelous way to eliminate stress. I remember my own first experience in a singing bar. I resisted heroically because I cannot carry a tune, don't know the words to any song, and am shy about making an utter fool of myself.

My Japanese hosts would not let me off the hook, however, and finally one of them agreed to join me in a duo. We were given a song book so I was able to struggle through. Despite the embarrassment, it was a very satisfying experience and I was immensely pleased with myself (the drunken audience applauded loudly).

You can avoid a great deal of the embarrassment I went through, have much more fun, and impress your Japanese contacts favorably by learning a couple of popular ballads and willingly belting them out with gusto at the first invitation.

47

Nomi-nication: Gathering Wisdom in Bars

Another facet of the Japanese custom of using cabarets and other *mizu shobai* facilities in their conduct of business is one that is described by the recently coined word "*nomi*-nica-tion." *Nomi* means "to drink" in Japanese. When combined with the latter half of "communication" you have a form of communicating through drinking.

As we have already learned, it is conventional wisdom in Japan that a person reveals his true self only when drunk and that you can get to really know a person only when they are in a state of inebriation. Given this situation, which is basically true in Japan because sober-time etiquette precludes "honest" behavior on other occasions, it is simply mandatory that the Japanese get together and drink in order to really get acquainted and find out what they actually think about things, business matters, or whatever.

In other words, if this situation is accepted as basically fact, the Japanese would not be able to suc-ceed in business without regularly hitting the bottle with their co-workers. Experience proves that it is true to some extent. Many Japanese businessmen have told me directly that their whole approach to maintaining effective employee relations, developing and using business contacts, and "gathering wisdom" was done through or while drinking.

Certainly not all Japanese businessmen go quite that far, but there is no doubt that "*nomi*-nication" is a vital part of the business process in Japan, and is therefore an important skill foreign businessmen should learn. Virtually all Japanese businessmen have two or three *ikitsuke no ba* (ee-kee-skay no bah), or "favorite bars," where they regularly take associates and guests for business conversations. It is recommended that foreign businessmen have their own *ikitsuke no ba* or clubs for the same purpose.

48

Let's Have a Drink

If you want to get acquainted with a Japanese businessman for whatever purpose, or have a "heart-to-heart" talk with a businessman you already know, neither your office nor his office is the place to do it. There are a number of reasons for this—one being that few Japanese businessmen have private offices, and holding such meetings in conference rooms is not appropriate. The most important reason, however, is that the "personal side" of business has traditionally been pursued outside the office—at coffee shops, restaurants, or bar-lounges (as opposed to cabarets).

A signal that someone wants to get to know you or talk to you seriously about anything, including business, is an invitation to meet outside the office. This invitation is often made in the form of the stock phrase *Ippai yarimasho!* (eep-pie yah-ree-mah-show).

This literally means "Let's do a full one (cup or glass)." In other words, "Let's have a drink." When addressing a foreigner, the invitation may be couched in more elegant terms.

This is an institutionalized facet of the business process in Japan, and one that you can also use. It is best done in the evening, and may include drinks and dinner or just drinks if it ends by around seven o'clock. The best places for such meetings are the lounges of hotels or private clubs.

Generally speaking, it is the lower- and middle-ranked managers who will most readily respond to such invitations (if they decline twice in a row you can assume you are not on their approved list). The closer you are to their age and rank, or if you are higher and there are no other negatives, the more likely they will accept such an invitation.

In the case of upper-level and top management it would not be considered appropriate for you to invite them out unless you are approximately the same age and rank. The higher the rank of the individual you invite out, the more prestigious the meeting place should be. Those in the upper stratosphere normally go only to private clubs or exclusive restaurants with private rooms for such meetings—not hotels.

If you have no choice but to use a hotel and your guest is to be someone of high rank in a major company or ministry, it would be appropriate to engage a private suite.

Many foreign businessmen stationed in Tokyo have found such after-hours meetings the ideal way to communicate on a very personal level with their Japanese counterparts.

49

Business on the Greens

There is another facet of doing business in Japan that is more familiar with Westerners, and generally more acceptable to them than the age-old *mizu shobai* approach—namely, cementing personal relations and doing business on the golf course. As soon as the Japanese in the late 1950s and 1960s became aware of the role of golf in business in the U.S., they took to it with the same obsessive dedication they exhibit toward any serious enterprise.

Membership in a golf course became an important business asset and a symbol of internationalism. Net-enclosed practice ranges sprang up on tiny vacant lots, on the tops of buildings, and in other unlikely places. Hundreds of thousands of Japanese men of all ages began spending part of their Sundays learning how to swing a golf club as part of their business skills.

For a present-day Japanese businessman to admit

that he does not belong to a golf club or does not play golf is like confessing to a serious failing in his professional training.

Although differing radically from the *mizu shobai,* particularly in that it is a Western practice and is far removed from traditional Japanese behavior, the golf course has nevertheless been integrated into the Japanese business system to a level on par with cabarets and geisha inns—providing Western businessmen with an opportunity to do business with the Japanese on equal if not advantageous terms.

A golf course is a golf course whether it is in or out of Japan. Being a Western game with its own rules of conduct based on individual action and behavior, golf (unlike baseball) cannot be Japanized. The foreign businessman does not have to know Japanese protocol to play golf with Japanese businessmen. On the contrary, it is they who must change their behavior.

Japanese businessmen who do business with foreigners generally have two "modes" of operation— a Japanese mode and a foreign mode. When they are dealing with foreigners, their attitudes and behavior undergo changes that range from subtle to drastic. When they are in their own offices in Japan, surrounded by their co-workers, these changes are very subtle, and often do not appreciably change the end result of their dealings with foreigners. The further they get away from their own office and co-workers, however, the more significant the change.

To the Japanese, cultural behavior is intimately related to physical surroundings. In a Japanese setting they will behave in a traditional Japanese way. In foreign settings, they tend to behave in the manner that they think is appropriate for that particular setting. Their behavior on a golf course in Japan—a Western setting—differs from their office behavior. Their behavior on a golf course outside of Japan differs even more, because the setting is more non-Japanese.

Foreign businessmen can take significant advantage of this chameleon factor in the Japanese character to help level the playing field when they engage in business with the Japanese. In other words, the more of your business talks and negotiations you can have outside the home office of the Japanese the better, and the more often these outside locations can be in Western settings the more advantage you will have.

Of course, I am not suggesting that you set up tables and chairs on a golf course and engage in full-fledged negotiations on the greens. But the golf course as well as other strictly Western scenarios are the foreign equivalent of the cabaret, where the Japanese way is to stop singing or grab-assing for just a few seconds or minutes to make their business position and/or requirements clear. These little business interludes should be well-planned and deliberately but deftly executed.

The idea is to shift your manner and behavior entirely for just the brief period that you are in a business mode, going from very casual to very serious. This sudden shift will alert the Japanese antenna that an important message is coming in, and since this is the way they operate, it should be loud and clear.

50

A Dash of Culture

It has been said that the religion of present-day Japan is business. But because of Japan's long association with Confucianism, Daoism, and Buddhism, there is a philosophical streak in most Japanese that begins to emerge and flower as they grow older. This philosophical bent is particularly evident in men, and seems to grow more pronounced the more successful they are.

The businessman-philosopher is certainly not unknown in the West, but he is the exception rather than the rule. In Japan, on the other hand, the final stage of virtually every successful businessman is that of a philosopher—as if the transformation was preordained. The nature of business management in Japan is a reflection of this phenomenon. The higher level executive is expected to withdraw more and more from daily company activities as he moves up the managerial ladder, and to become a sage—the company's philosophical and spiritual guide.

The historical traditions of the West as well as contemporary management practices, in particular the musical-chairs movement of executives among companies, generally precludes the development of the type of loyalty and security that is necessary to inspire and sustain a philosophical concern for either company or country. Western businessmen are therefore apt to be handicapped in their dealings with the Japanese.

One of the ways to mitigate this weakness is to inject a conspicuously cultural element into your business relationships with the Japanese. This element may involve art, handicrafts, music, literature, other cultural expressions, or combinations of them. Such concern and involvement lowers the obsession with material things, and puts the practice of business on a higher and more personal level—all things that the Japanese appreciate and believe to be morally right.

One American businessman stationed in Japan for many years gained a lot of mileage with his Japanese counterparts as the result of becoming a collector of pottery and something of an authority on its history in Japan. This alone took him out of the admittedly stereotyped image of the foreign businessman in Japan, and gave him a cultural tie with the Japanese that helped him transcend the differences that separated them.

Another foreign businessman of my acquaintance achieved the same results from his interest and involvement in woodblock prints. Still another turned a strong interest in the writings of contemporary Japanese businessmen into a valuable asset in his business relationships in Japan (reaching the point where he was invited to lecture on the differences between Japanese and foreign management practices, thus vastly increasing his network of contacts within the Japanese community).

This cultural element does not have to be Japanese although it is usually more effective when it is, simply because the Japanese can immediately relate to it. One exception worth mentioning was the Texas businessman whose collection of cowboy artifacts—plus his down-to-earth cowboy personality—was sufficiently fascinating to the Japanese to earn him their respect and enthusiastic cooperation in business.

51

And a Pinch of Sex

As is obvious from the size and importance of the *mizu shobai* in Japan, which is based on the sexual attraction between males and females as well as the social lubrication provided by drinking together, sex is one of the keys to successful business in Japan. As camouflaged as it might be, and as different as it might be from the heydays of the great legal red-light districts and ubiquitous brothel inns of pre-1956 Japan, sex remains a key ingredient in establishing as well as sustaining business relationships in Japan.

Foreign businessmen wanting to do business with the Japanese should be aware of the sexual factor— they can hardly ignore it if they go to Japan—and have the option of using it in Japan or in their home country. In Japan this involves becoming acquainted with the managers of two or three cabarets where you are welcome and can take Japanese guests, and, if you represent a larger company that can afford the tab, two or three *ryotei* (rio-tay-e) or Japanese-style restaurant inns where geisha can be called in. You may also want to establish "face" at a soapland.

The managers of most of the smaller, more intimate lounge-type cabarets where it is best to take Japanese guests are usually women who were formerly hostesses. Given the nature of the business, they are invariably very friendly, expert at dealing with men out for a good time, and themselves often still very attractive. It is usually necessary to have an introduction to them from a valued Japanese or foreign patron, and then to patronize the place on a regular basis over a period of several months to establish the necessary kind of relationship. This means they recognize you by face and name, greet you enthusiastically when you arrive, allow their best-looking and most popular hostesses to serve you, and allow you to pay your bill by the month if you wish (the Japanese are impressed when a foreigner has established credit at a cabaret and can walk out without so much as a mention of money).

One of the primary reasons for establishing a personal relationship with cabaret managers is to make sure the fees you pay are not more than the going rate for regular Japanese patrons. This is very important because generally speaking cabarets do not operate on the basis of fixed menu prices—which is why I say "fees" instead of "charges." There are generally understood hourly rates for the company of hostesses and there may be a door or table charge that can be quoted to you, and if you ask how much a beer costs there is usually an answer, but the final bill is not based on what you drank or ate but how many guests you have in your party, on how long you stayed in the club and how many girls joined your party during your stay, multiplied by the club's base rate for each.

For example, if there are four people in your party, you are serviced by only four girls and stay for two hours, your bill might be sixty thousand yen. If six girls join your party during the same period, the bill will probably be fifteen to twenty thousand yen more. What you must do in advance, if the person who introduced you does not tell you, is to ask the manager to give you ball park figures per guest per hour per girl.

The variable factor that throws uninitiated foreigners is the system of rotating girls among the tables. If you do not establish a limit, a dozen or more girls may alternately join your party for fifteen or twenty minutes each, running your bill up to astonishing figures (in the more unscrupulous places this is often done deliberately, with each girl being credited with an hour's time even though she may be at your table for just a few minutes).

Foreigners who, new to the system, wander into cabaret-lounges on their own and do not settle on a fee in advance, are frequently over-charged.

Japan's *ryotei,* which are what foreigners have traditionally described as "geisha houses," are in fact very private and very exclusive Japanese-style inns, with reed-mat floors and sliding paper doors, that serve meals in private rooms and call in geisha for patrons who want their services.

Ryotei are not open to the walk-in public. You must have reservations in all cases, and in the more prestigious places you must have an introduction from a known and approved patron and make your reservations well in advance. In addition to serving evening meals at geisha-catered parties, the inns also act as discreet houses of assignation for daytime or nighttime trysts. Rates per person and per hour vary with the inn. Inquiries in advance are essential.

Neither the cabaret nor the *ryotei* engage in outright sex for sale, but are part of the system that contributes to the sensual side of business in Japan. Geisha are almost never available as sex partners except to well-established patrons (many geisha are too ugly and too old to be sexually attractive), but inn patrons may bring in other female partners. Cabaret hostesses who are single (and they generally are) do not work as prostitutes but typically develop sexual liaisons with favored patrons some time during their careers. Some carry on affairs with more than one patron at the same time. Others, particularly those who have formed relationships with well-to-do businessmen who shower them with gifts and money, remain faithful mistresses.

As mentioned earlier, there is a close relationship between the personal nature of business in Japan and the sexual connotations of the *mizu shobai,* a relationship that works just as well outside of Japan. The foreign businessman who wants to add the sexual ingredient to his relationship with his Japanese counterparts during their visits from Japan, can do so by taking them to the foreign equivalent of the *mizu shobai*—bars, clubs, or other places where young, attractive women are available as companions or partners.

Just as most foreign men find Japanese girls exceptionally attractive sensually, Japanese men are turned on by young, attractive foreign women, particularly blue-eyed, busty blondes who are the epitome of exotic feminine sensuality to Japanese men. In the old days in Japan, two men going to a brothel together created a special bond between them. The ultimate was for them to have the same woman. Times have changed, of course, but the tradition lingers.

52

When the Going Gets Tough

The typical foreign businessman going into his first relationship with a Japanese company is apt to sigh with relief and lower his guard once a contract is signed. That is often premature. The Japanese do not regard a contract as something that is chiseled in stone, to be followed precisely to the letter. A contract in the Japanese sense is an agreement to work together. Of course, there may be provisions that are clearly meant to be followed exactly, but in general they see contracts as guidelines, with a lot of flexibility regardless of the small print.

This attitude goes back to the basic fact that the Japanese do not see things as black or white, as absolutely right or wrong. They see things in many shades, depending on circumstances, and believe that it is right and proper to change both their attitudes and behavior with circumstances. This is why prominent critics of the Japanese frequently say they do not have

principles, they have policies. It is also why so many
"right or wrong" Westerners are often confused by
Japanese behavior and have difficulty understanding
them.

As a result of this cultural way, foreign businessmen often encounter more problems with their
Japanese partners after contracts have been signed
than before—especially when the relationships are intimate ones, in Japan, and require daily contact and
regular decisions. Invariably there will be differences
of judgement on what should be done as well as how to
do it. One side has to give in or a compromise has to
be worked out.

The relationship may work well enough and even
exceptionally well when the synergy between the two
parties happens to mesh and become more than the
sum of one plus one. But the possibility of the relationship becoming a contest of power is more likely to happen. In that case, whether or not the relationship
succeeds is determined by the caliber of the managers
on both sides. Overall, management must be wise
enough to recognize the sources of friction and, like
the judo master, use the weight, energy, and strength
of each side to move the project forward despite their
differences.

Obviously circumstances do change, often on a
daily basis, and it is up to the foreign side to recognize
that the Japanese rationale may be just as valid as
their own—if not more so—and be prepared to accom-

modate themselves to it. At the same time, a warning is in order. The man whose actions are based on policies instead of principles frequently has an advantage over the man of principle. The man of policy can change his actions to give him an advantage, when the man of principle would be prevented from making similar changes.

In the past, Japan as a nation, and individual Japanese as well, have often given policy precedence over principle (as most nations and people frequently do), and certainly not always for selfish or unfair or insidious reasons. The practice is woven deep in the fabric of Japanese culture. In day-to-day business affairs with others who play according to different rules, the advantage can tilt the game in their favor.

Follow-up after a contract is signed is just as important as during the getting acquainted and negotiating processes, and often requires more expertise and persistence because prior to the signing the Japanese participants were on their best behavior.

53

Why the Japanese Are Quality Conscious

In the 1970s Japanese businessmen and politicians often commented that they learned quality control from the Americans (and then turned the tables on them by doing it better). It is true that the principles of statistical quality control in manufacturing were given to Japan just after the end of World War II by Dr. W. E. Deming (who was totally ignored by American businessmen until the mid-1980s), and a further significant contribution was made by Dr. J. M. Juran in 1954, but it was not as if the Japanese were starting from scratch in quality consciousness.

The reputation that the Japanese had prior to World War II and in the first two decades following the end of the war was a historical fluke that resulted from the demands of foreign importers—not the inclinations or habits of Japanese manufacturers or exporters.

Soon after the U.S. forced feudal Japan to open its doors to the Western world in the 1850s, and following the downfall of the last shogunate in 1868, large numbers of foreign importers began flocking to Japan with their product samples to place orders for a variety of consumer goods, ranging from toys to textiles. These foreign buyers were attracted to Japan because labor was cheap and because the Japanese were diligent workers, highly skilled in duplicating samples brought to them by American and European importers.

By the early 1900s the Japanese had the reputation of being the greatest copiers and imitators in the world. They could and would copy anything foreign importers brought to them. Very little of this imitation foreign merchandise was sold in Japan, however. They regarded it with contempt; as something only unsophisticated, uncultured foreigners would buy, and referred to it derisively as *Yokohama-hin* (Yokohama heen), or ''Yokohama goods,'' since most of it was shipped out of Japan through the port of Yokohama.

As soon as World War II ended in 1945, foreign importers once again began clamoring to get back into Japan. By the early 1950s, Japan's hotels were bulging at the seams with American and European buyers loaded down with samples they wanted copied in Japan. The biggest contingent of these bargain-hunting buyers were from New York City. By 1958 all of the major American department store chains had buying offices in Tokyo or Osaka. The Sears Roebuck buying office in Tokyo had a staff of more than sixty people.

The system was simple. Foreign buyers would carry in samples of products they wanted copied in Japan and bring as much pressure as possible on Japanese makers to get the lowest prices possible. The Japanese were hungry and had no choice if they wanted to survive. For about ten years foreign importers controlled most of what was produced in Japan as well as its quality and price.

Gradually during the last half of the 1950s and then with a rush in the early 1960s, the Japanese began to take control of their export industries. They began coming up with product designs of their own, establishing their own network of buyers abroad, raising the quality level of their merchandise, and resisting the blandishments of foreign importers to continue making cheap imitations.

As they became stronger, Japanese manufacturers began opening sales offices abroad, bypassing not only Japanese exporters but their American and European importers as well. Within a span of about five years Sony and dozens of other soon-to-be-famous Japanese makers broke with their foreign distributors and set up their own distribution networks in the U.S. and elsewhere. By the 1970s most of the Japanese merchandise being imported into the United States and Europe was not being imported by American or European companies. It was being imported by the branch offices of *Japanese* companies. And the quality of Japanese-made merchandise was widely regarded as the best in the world.

The Japanese were not strangers to quality products. Far from it. They had a history of nearly two thousand years during which their master-apprentice system in the handicrafts and arts produced one generation after another of some of the finest artists and craftsmen in the world. The appreciation of beauty in the ordinary products of life became a cult.

This tradition was ignored by the waves of foreign traders who descended upon Japan from the 1860s to the 1960s, but the Japanese were to have their day—or their century! One of the many challenges now facing most of the rest of the world is how to compete with Japan in both quality and productivity. An appreciation for quality is deeply ingrained in Japanese culture, and is not something we can easily imitate. It is a fundamental thing that goes to the roots of our own philosophy and life-style. Until this is recognized, and something basic is done about it, we will continue to take a back seat to the Japanese where quality is concerned.

54

The *Kaizen* Factor

The Japanese obsession with quality is spurred by a newly evolved cultural concept known as *kaizen* (kie-zen), which can be translated directly as ''change for the better'' and refers to modifications that are desirable. The word itself is apparently an old one, but in feudal Japan, which did not officially end until 1868, change in fact was not fashionable. For some two hundred and fifty years the shogunate government did its best to keep things as they were—and had been for centuries.

Because of this official policy, there was a pent-up

demand for change when anti-shogun forces finally toppled the feudal government in the 1860s, unleashing a frenzy of importing and synthesizing foreign ideas. At the same time, the artistry and merit of purely Japanese things was downgraded.

It was to be almost one hundred years before the Japanese were to merge the traditions of quality in their domestic arts and crafts with foreign-style products, and astound the world. Part of this process was adoption of the concept implied in the word *kaizen*, virtually making it into a cult, and applying it to the manufacturing process from step one. In this context, the Japanese are never satisfied with the quality of product and are constantly analyzing every aspect of the design, every step of production, in an attempt to achieve absolute perfection.

Having seen the success of their extraordinary drive for quality and the remarkable economic progress that has resulted from it, the Japanese say that the spirit of *kaizen* (now translated as "continual improvement") has permeated their entire culture, and that they are now totally imbued with the need to make continuous improvement an integral part of their daily work.

While this claim is obviously overstated, it is nevertheless true enough to give the Japanese a significant advantage in the competition for world markets, and is one of the keys foreign businessmen must clearly understand and learn how to use. The days when a philosophy of "minimum acceptable quality" was enough to get by on are long gone. The new standard, which Japan has set, is "the highest possible quality."

55

The Art of Servicing Customers

Customer service is another area in which the Japanese excel, and is one more thing that must be on the list of anyone wanting to succeed in business in Japan.

The Japanese traditions of customer service, like most other aspects of their outlook and behavior, are deeply rooted in their history. From the beginning down to modern times, Japanese society was based on a finely tuned hierarchical structure. People were divided into highly distinguishable classes and ranks within classes, and there was a very specific and very harshly enforced etiquette for each class and rank.

The behavior of inferiors toward superiors was prescribed. The higher the personage in class and rank, the more precise the behavior and the more carefully it was designed to exalt the superior person. Given human nature, higher ranking individuals got used to being effusively catered to by underlings, who in turn were conditioned to provide the kind of service expected and demanded.

Over the centuries the concept and practice of a highly refined and stylized form of service gradually permeated Japanese society from top to bottom. Eventually all guests were treated in the same or similar manner as high-ranking superiors. Finally, it became the rule for customers as well to be given the same kind of royal treatment. In fact, it became the custom to refer to customers as *O-Kyaku San* (oh-kyack sahn) or "Mr. (or Mrs.) Honorable Guest."

While considerably diluted in present-day Japan, the age-old custom of treating customers as honored guests is still the bedrock of customer service and is a vitally important aspect of business management. It is expected and typical of Japanese retail shops, wholesalers, and makers that they provide a conspicuously high degree and quality of before-and-after service to their customers.

Not surprisingly, the foreign businessman wanting to succeed in Japan must provide the kind and quality of service consumers naturally expect.

56

Putting on a Loving Face

Another facet of Japanese behavior that is especially conspicuous in business, particularly on the retail-consumer level, is one that is called *aiso* (aye-so), which might be translated as "loving care." *Aiso* refers to a person's facial expression and overall manner.

The Japanese not only demand good service when they go into a store, restaurant, or other place of business, they want a "loving care" expression and manner from the people who wait on them.

Anyone who has been to Japan has witnessed—and heard—innumerable times the reaction of restaurant staff and others in the consumer business when customers come in and leave. Not everyone manages to have loving care smiles on their faces, but the enthusiastic welcomes to arriving customers and expressions of gratitude to departing customers make up for it.

This is an age-old custom that is part of the Japanese concept of service, and one they point to with pride when listing all the areas in which Japan is superior to other countries. Of course, much of this kind of behavior is just good sense—having a pleasant look on your face when a customer comes in, greeting him enthusiastically and then thanking him profusely when he leaves is just good public relations. But again it is polished to a high art in Japan.

Most foreign businessmen who have set up retail businesses in Japan soon learned the wisdom of giving the customers what they want. It is a principle that travels well, and could easily be adopted outside of Japan.

57

Grinding Sesame Seeds

The foreigner who wants to succeed in doing business with the Japanese should know and become an expert at *goma suri* (go-mah suu-ree), which literally means "grinding sesame seeds."

This is a term used in reference to one of the techniques the Japanese have developed to maintain harmonious personal relations in spite of the formal, demanding nature of their etiquette. There are so many rules of conduct, and people tend to be so sensitive to slights, that most Japanese spend a significant proportion of their time involved in *goma suri*.

Probably the most used tools in the *goma suri* process are compliments and praise, among themselves as well as to foreigners. In fact, foreigners come in for an exceptional amount of praise in Japan because of a strong Japanese desire to appear friendly. Demonstrating the slightest ability with chopsticks or using a few words or sentences of Japanese is invariably enough to elicit effusive compliments.

Responding with proper humility to this kind of behavior and using it at appropriate times will help smooth your way.

A word of caution: in a company situation, paying compliments to young women whom you know only casually can be taken far more seriously than you might intend. The Japanese have no taboos against courting and catching women. But such fun is strictly relegated to its place outside of the office.

58

Making Hay in the Japanese Market

All things considered, it is probably more difficult to successfully market a product in Japan than anywhere else in the world. Among the reasons for this: advertising and marketing services tend to be more expensive; the large number and numerous levels of distributors and wholesalers create a maze-like barrier that adds to the cost; and the huge number of retail outlets—over 1.7 million—present both an extraordinary potential and a formidable obstacle. But in many ways the biggest barrier of all is the Japanese consumer.

The Japanese are probably the world's most discriminating and demanding consumers, and are surely the best informed. They expect and demand quality down to a minute level. A shirt with a piece of thread hanging out is not acceptable. A product on which the inside is not as perfectly finished as the outside is regarded as a reject. A badly designed product is not likely to go anywhere unless it is badly needed and there is no other choice—and the Japanese recognize good and bad design when they see it.

The Japanese really care about what they buy. When they are considering making a purchase they do not think "Where can I get the lowest price?" Their question is "Where can I get the best product?"

Another Japanese trait that throws many foreign companies wanting to market their goods in Japan is their insistence on high-quality packaging. One might be tempted to call them spoiled, but for a thousand years or more packaging in Japan has been an art form, getting as much attention as the products themselves. Japanese businessmen surely spend a larger amount on professional package design than anyone else, and it shows.

To compete in the Japanese market the foreign product generally has to be both designed for and specifically packaged for the market. The publicity and promotion must be carefully crafted to appeal to the subtle, sophisticated tastes of the Japanese, with all the currently sanctioned nuances right on.

The refinements necessary to meet the demands of the Japanese marketplace, from basic design to packaging, can generally be achieved only by a highly experienced *Japanese* staff. About the only foreign-created packaging that has been successful in Japan have been some French and Italian designs. This means the foreign businessman contemplating launching a consumer product in Japan must be as concerned about the expertise of his Japanese staff and suppliers as he is with his product.

Keys to entering the Japanese consumer market successfully include thorough research up front, especially becoming familiar with the distribution and retailing systems in your product area, obtaining copious input and direction from local recognized, recommended experts, and obtaining the services of a thoroughly experienced Japanese manager.

59

Going After the Young

If there is one general rule that foreign businessmen should follow in their efforts to penetrate the Japanese market it is "go after the young." The youth of Japan constitute one of the richest and most exciting markets in the world.

Social surveys show that the attitudes and behavior of Japan's urban young—those born after 1965—are so different from what is generally perceived as "Japanese" behavior that they are indeed a "new breed," as they have been labeled.

To succeed in the market of the young requires an intimate knowledge of their lifestyles and the forces that are leading them—fashions, new foods, recreation, and entertainment—and this is one area where foreign businessmen have an advantage over their Japanese counterparts, if they will pick up on it.

The new kind of consumer that Japan's youth have become and are becoming is strictly Western, and American in particular. More and more, they are looking like and acting like Americans, responding to the same motivations and advertising appeals. So drastic are the changes in Japan's ''new breed'' that older Japanese businessmen can no longer stay on top of the market using their bellies, the universal mind, or any form of traditional cultural wisdom.

The days when Japan's manufacturers could depend on the homogeneity and predictability of the youth segment of market, and do no product research at all, are gone. American and European marketers, with their decades of experience in the volatile youth field, have a definite edge over the old line Japanese firms that have traditionally dominated the home market, and should take advantage of it.

Tokyo marketing consultant Dr. Jeanne Binstock has noted that the youth of Japan are more interested in communication than in tranquility, that they want action and richness in their lives, that they want personal achievement, and that they have become ''perfect consumers.''

60

From Zen to Xenophobia

 I have mentioned that many
Japanese Japanese are generally uncomfortable in any
involvement with Westerners and that businessmen
and tradespeople as well as influential opinion makers
will frequently say that they simply do not like *gaijin*
(guy-jeen), which literally means "outside person"
and is the Japanese word for "foreigner." Another
group of Japanese who frequently express the same
sentiment are low-level gangsters or hoods.

This leaves a very large segment of the Japanese
population who are either neutral or readily admit to
liking foreigners (as much as they do anyone else),
and, interestingly, the majority of this group are
women.

The origin of the xenophobia that afflicts so many
Japanese men is not hard to understand. The small,
relatively isolated islands, the exclusivity of the
culture, ignorance of the world at large, a deep-rooted
inferiority complex mixed with an equally strong
superiority complex, a fear of the predatory nature of
other systems—all have shaped their attitudes. And,
of course, xenophobia exists everywhere, but usually

not to the extent or in the manner that it does in Japan.

My reason for bringing it up here is that it is prevalent enough that it impacts on Japan's economic as well as its social and political attitudes and policies, and therefore on the interests of other countries. Japanese xenophobia makes itself felt in most business relationships with outsiders. So far, the characteristic has obviously not harmed Japan economically. In fact, it has been part of the motivation for some of the trade barriers that protect Japan from foreign competition. As such, it has harmed foreign businessmen doing business with or attempting to do business with Japan.

On a personal level, it is very common for foreigners in Japan looking for apartments or homes to rent to be turned down because they are not Japanese. The majority of Japanese companies will not hire foreign employees in Japan because of racial and cultural factors. Numerous bars and other nightspots around the country have a "No Foreigners" policy.

It is still news when a well-known domestic Japanese company breaks the barrier and hires a foreigner as a full-time regular employee—and when it does it is often a reaction to outside pressure and is more of a face-saving gesture than anything else. The exceptions to date have been a few department stores and securities companies. Generally, Japanese do not make any attempt to conceal their prejudices. They regard them as natural.

It is becoming more and more obvious that Japan must internationalize its economy in order to contribute to more harmony and reciprocity in world markets, and to do that, its society—the fabric of its culture—must also change. The only way this change is going to come about, at the speed and to the degree that it should and must, is for Japan's trading partners to continue pressuring it—a point that my Japanese friends and colleagues have been repeating over and over since the 1970s. And that means pressure from individual businessmen as well as from foreign governments.

The rationale of the people who continue to individually and privately appeal for more pressure from the outside to force Japan to changes its predatory and unfair trading policies is that the *natto* structure and nature of major companies and the government make it impossible for them to change from the inside.

But for some perverse reason, perhaps a sense of guilt or maybe their own cross-cultural inadequacies, foreign political leaders as well as businessmen have let the Japanese walk all over them; have let them play by their rules. I believe that individual foreign businessmen can help remedy this situation by constantly pressuring their Japanese counterparts to live up to their obligations to help internationalize Japan—something virtually all admit must be done. I recommend that foreign businessmen going in with new products and projects emphasize that it is imperative that Japan's trade and investment be two ways, and that what you are proposing will make a contribution.

The Japanese *are* receptive to personal and emotional appeals when it comes to the survival and future benefit of their country, and by tying this in with your own business relationship you can put yourself on the high road, as seeking to benefit Japan as well as yourself and your own country.

61

More Mistakes Foreigners Make

Probably one of the most common "mistakes" many foreign businessmen in Japan make results from an inability to communicate in Japanese. Not being able to speak or understand Japanese, they naturally gravitate to those Japanese who speak English because they have no other practical choice. While helping to eliminate some problems, this often creates more problems than it solves.

It often happens that the people who speak English are not key individuals in the hierarchy of rank. It is also commonplace for these people to be resented, sometimes strongly, by the Japanese who cannot communicate in English. Foreigners easily get into the habit of going directly to the English speakers without attaching very much importance to their actions, but in doing so they may be exposing themselves and their English-speaking contacts to all kinds of jeopardy.

First, this situation automatically puts the English speakers in a key position as far as both the foreign and Japanese side are concerned—neither side can function without using them as go-betweens. In addition to usually being younger than the managers who have to use them, these people are also often relatively new and inexperienced in the company, and quite often speaking English is their only skill. While essential cogs in the foreign-Japanese relationship, they often complicate matters because of their lack of experience and knowledge in professional and technical areas of business.

American businessmen in particular tend to treat this group of people as equals, presume they are smart and capable because they speak English, and do not distinguish between them and the higher-ranking, much more important members of the Japanese company. In fact, because they are often completely dependent upon them, foreigners sometimes appear to be ignoring the other Japanese. To the non-English-speaking Japanese managers, this is thoughtless and rude.

Foreign businessmen put into this situation because of their inability to speak Japanese should be acutely aware of the sensitivity of their Japanese counterparts and learn how to "use" other people as interpreters without slighting those they are talking to. The first step in this is to force yourself to face the individual concerned and talk directly to him or her—not talk "to" the interpreter.

Another mistake that foreigners frequently make in their approaches to Japanese companies—and alluded to earlier—is attempting to conduct all of their dealings with the highest-ranking executives. In larger Japanese companies top-level executives generally do not get involved in the early stages of a project, however large.

The preferred approach is to have an introduction to a ranking executive, and then after you have introduced yourself, gone through the diplomatic niceties, and stated your business in broad terms, ask him to introduce you to the proper department head *(bucho)*, who will then bring in other middle-level managers to hear you out and decide whether to make recommendations to upper management to pursue your project. Again, the key people in researching potential new projects are usually on the section *(ka)* level, with the *kacho* (section chiefs) reporting their findings to the department manager.

An important aspect of working effectively with a Japanese company is to ask enough questions to show that you know who is who and how their particular system works. The more you take for granted, the more likely you will run into trouble.

62

I Will Do My Best

A cultural trap that many foreign politicians, diplomats, and businessmen have stepped into in their dealings with Japan is bound up in the common expression *zensho shimasu* (zen-show she-mahss), which is sometimes translated as "I will do my best," and other times as "I will take care of it."

The meaning intended when this phrase is used is not always clear from the context of the conversation, and therein lies the rub. A person who is asked to do something may respond enthusiastically with *zensho shimasu*. If the hearer accepts this as meaning "I will take care of it," while the speaker means "I will do my best," both parties may be confused as well as put out by the mutual misunderstandings that can occur.

A Japanese speaker will use the "I will do my best" version of *zensho shimasu* when he knows full well that he cannot or doesn't intend to do anything, without intending to deceive the other party. What he does do is leave it up to the other party to divine his real meaning and the reasons why he responded with this ambiguous term, and accept them without getting mad.

This is another situation where the foreign businessman who is not truly plugged into the Japanese wavelength may have trouble decoding the message. It is also a regular custom for Japanese to just begin a sentence and leave two-thirds or more of it unsaid for the listener to fill in. Given this added aspect of communicating in Japan, you must at all times go the extra mile in making sure that you are understanding and being understood by your Japanese contacts and associates.

63

I Understand You

Here is another of those common Japanese phrases over which one can stumble and fall. I have put it at the end of my abbreviated list of keys for doing business in Japan not because it is the least important key, but because it is so basic that it should always be uppermost in your mind.

It is a cultural habit of the Japanese to say, *Hai, wakarimasu* (Hie, wah-kah-ree-mahss), "Yes, I understand," or the past tense, *Hai, wakarimashita* (Hie, wah-kah-ree-mahssh-tah), "I understood (what you said)." The foreigner, unfortunately, can mistake this as an affirmative response *and believe that some action* is going to be initiated. There are occasions when this phrase means the same in English as it does in Japanese. There are other occasions when it *does* mean that the individual responding is going to do what he was told to do or what he was asked to consider (and do).

Often, when foreigners make presentations or request things, Japanese will respond with this phrase when it just means that they heard and understood—not that they were going to do anything. On these occasions, using the term is another way of delaying things or brushing them aside altogether. And the meaning is the same whether it is said in Japanese or English.

The challenge, of course, is to interpret the response correctly. If it is in fact an affirmative reply and action is going to be taken, you can usually determine this by an additional question or two regarding time or scheduling. At this point, if the response is unclear or noncommittal you have your answer.

64

A Final Point

While Michihiro Matsumoto's *natto* company analogy is very useful in helping newcomers get the idea that Japanese companies are different and must be approached and dealt with differently, I believe the next step is to look at every Japanese company of any size as a political democracy.

In larger companies the president or chairman of the board may appear to be all-powerful, but actually his authority is mostly an illusion. Generally, he cannot or will not do anything that is not approved by the directors. The directors and other top executives, like members of Congress, have to depend on coalitions and cooperation from other directors to get anything done—and they are vulnerable to pressure from "lobbyists."

The people who "run" a Japanese company (with the advice and consent of the president and directors), on whom the president and directors depend, are the department heads (*bucho*) and section heads (*kacho*), whose role is similar to that of government bureaucrats. Just as bureaucrats generally have the last word in democratic countries, so do the *bu/kacho* in Japanese companies.

Establishing and maintaining a working relationship with a Japanese company follows the same pattern as dealing with a country, protocol and all—constantly gathering intelligence, engaging in diplomacy on the highest level, conducting an ongoing public relations program, nurturing close working ties with the actual managers, and constantly adjusting the relationship to keep up with the tides of change.

When you present yourself to a Japanese company, you want your credentials in order, your knowledge of the right protocol polished to a high sheen, your intelligence right on, your advisors in the wings, and your troops lined up.

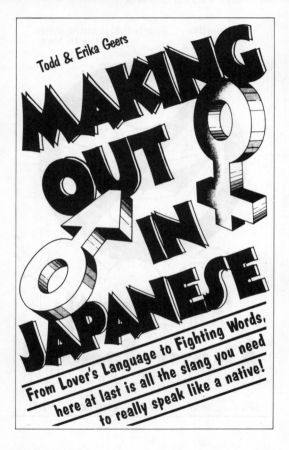

ISBN 0-8048-1541-0

¥590 / $5.95

YENBOOKS